Raising Sane

Is It Possible to Raise a Sane Child in an Insane World

By

Edward W. Jones

Transcriptions by **Dona Bilangi**

Editing by **Marilyn Meadors**

ISBN: 978-0-9844269-3-5

Library of Congress Control Number:
2014952239

Publisher

Reality Source, Arkansas, USA

Printed in the United States

Table of Contents

Preface i

Introduction iii

A World of Illusion 1

Knowing Nothing 5

Transformation Ends Conditioning 8

Children's Sensitivity 11

We Live in a Violent World 14

Forming a Partnership 16

Consequences vs. Punishment 19

Breaking Patterns 23

Seeing vs. Knowing 26

The Gift of Failure 29

Breaking the Chains 32

Raising Your Inner Child 34

The World's Worst 36

Developing Images 38

The Action of Creation 40

Transformation—A New Beginning 42

Being 100 Percent Responsible 44

Creating a Partnership with a Child 46

Creating a Partnership with Yourself 49

Discover Yourself in Relationship 53

Death of the Ego 55

Life Lives in Questions 56

Ending Ties that Bind 58

Bailing Out Children 61

We Are Still Children 63

End Doing Things for Them 66

A Child's Imagination 68

Developing Games for Children 70

Success or Failure—A New Look 73

Taking Care of Adult Children 76

Weed Your Mind 79

Learning the Lies 82
Want Is a Four-Letter Word 84
"Yes" or "No" 90
Being Attuned to Your Child 94
Living Your Labels 97
World Peace 105
Labeled by Schools and Doctors 108
See the Lies 111
The Need to Be Right 114
End the Insanity 116
Keeping Your Word 120
Be Free—The Good-Bye Exercise 122
No Excuses 127
Stand Up and Get Moving 129

Preface

In 1979, I experienced a four-hour long death of my consciousness. When it was over, I was not the person I was before it happened. The person who arose from the ashes of that death had been born new, born into a new consciousness which was absent of everything I had been— a hondo, macho man who thought he could whip the world. In his place was a person who knew nothing but still had to function in the world.

I could hear people clearly. In hearing what they were saying, I discovered they were manifesting their lives with what they were saying. I saw then that we bring forth our lives from the spoken word. We either invent our lives from thought processes passed down for thousands of years, or we create something new from not already knowing. Intelligence doesn't already know, and intelligence is not yet operating on the planet.

What we say, the words we use and the tone in which we deliver them are what determine the manner in which we will live our lives, and when the truth of that is seen, energy is delivered to the one who speaks the truth. A truth spoken begins to unravel all the lies we have been living for centuries.

Within these pages, I will ask you to speak many things to yourself or to others, and you may at first resist, or you may speak them silently to yourself. Just know that verbalization carries more energy and reward than speaking silently or writing the words. This is a book of doing.

When we hold our words inside of us and don't speak them, they turn to garbage. They give us diseases, both mentally and physically. Verbalization is the way to get it all out, and speaking creates the possibility for us to see if

i

what is spoken is true. The intent here is to dissolve the ego so that we can become real, live human beings. Only an ego can be hurt by words.

It is up to you whether you do these things I set forth for you to do, for some of them may be contrary to your beliefs and may be things that you think are negative. However, this is what I say needs to be done in order not to continue the manner in which we live on this planet, which is like robots just repeating our past. The words may seem too harsh for you to speak, but it is facing the sometimes harsh and ugly truth of self that will set you free, if free is your intent.

—Edward Jones

Introduction

You may be a parent caring to raise a child differently in a difficult and violent world, or you may be interested in a self-transformation. You will find both of these topics inextricably linked in this book. You will be introduced to actions you can take to alter the course of your life which will alter the course of your children's lives, and that will alter the course of the planet.

Pogo, a cartoon character, said in the 1960s during a time of war "we have met the enemy and he is us." We need to see that we are what the world is, and this world is encased in a stream of insanity. So if you are looking to raise a sane child in an insane world, you will need to look to yourself as well as the child. This is a discovery of a "what you can do book" to raise both your own inner child and your children out of insane and into sane—a transformation.

Edward Jones speaks of not already knowing what to do because "doing what we have always done has brought us to the brink of destroying ourselves and the planet on which we live. We will either transform, or more than likely we will perish." Edward states that his spontaneous transformation catapulted him to the place of creation, truth and love from where intelligent action can be created. Let us consider this book to be a discourse on intelligent actions.

Perhaps in reading these words something will grab your attention, and you will get an *ah-ha* moment, a jolt of awareness. If you can be a receiver of what is introduced in this book, you might see that you live in a stream of insanity, a stream that has been moving for thousands of years. You will then see it is time for that stream to end so as not to pass it on to your children.

A World of Illusion

Children are born pristine without belief. Then they are trained and conditioned by their parents and others around them to believe the same beliefs the parents were taught to believe. This has been going on for thousands of years. We are conditioned robots believing and repeating those ancient beliefs. We have accepted them as truth, and we will fight to the death to defend them.

Children think all the things they have been told are true, and they have stored those beliefs in their memories as truth. They are only stories told for eons which we all still hold onto. Then we teach our children to live in the made-up stories. We bring them up to believe the lies we tell them starting with Santa Clause, Easter bunnies, tooth fairies, and a god that punishes them if they don't believe. This goes on and on until they end up in the insanity of belief.

We live in this world of insanity. This is a thought invented world made up of belief and lies, and we have accepted it. Our thinking is not original. This kind of thinking has been passed down to us for generations, and then we fill our children with the same thinking. The invention of so many differing beliefs in the world and accepted by 99 percent of the human race has resulted in our species living in the domain of illusion—insanity.

So the goal, if we were to call it a goal, to raising a sane or transformed child would require having sane or transformed parents raising the child. That child would have a 50 percent greater possibility for remaining sane on the planet than the child whose parents live in illusion. Even if the child did have transformed parents, the child is still sent out into the world, and the world is made up of people also stuck in belief. The child will get insanity there as well.

The crux of the problem is that we as mothers and fathers haven't yet discovered we are part of an insane world, that we live as an illusion rather than a real entity. An illusion is the label we put on things and people. We label the female as *mother* and the male as *father*, and for the rest of our lives we try to live up to the meanings we give to those labels. Those words are not who we are; they are not the real entities, yet they are the framework in which we are living. People are the real entity, and when we attach labels to them, we develop an image and that is how we see them from then on. In other words, we have lost the ability to see the real person without the thoughts we have about them.

Let's start at the beginning. We notice that a child is either a male or female. The illusion begins when we add the label *boy* or *girl*. When someone says the word *boy* or *girl*, we get a specific image in our mind as to what the word means to us. Perhaps it is that boys wear blue; girls wear pink. These images are attached in our memory as labels. As children grow up they accumulate thousands of labels in every aspect of their lives, and these labels are all illusions. That continues throughout their lives.

Labels for the purpose of conversation might have a role for differentiation and explanations, and all of these labels do keep some order. The problem comes in when we get stuck in the labels by identifying with them and adding other labels to already existing labels. A mother wants to be a *good mother*, so she is starting out already in an illusion— the label of *mother*. No matter what she does, she will never be a good mother to some people based on all possible definitions of what a good mother is. For example, if you raised your child as a non-Christian, then to a Christian you are not a good mother.

When we are seeking to be good at anything, we will also bring along the bad with it. In the domain of duality, good/bad always go together. When we place the label or judgment of *good* or *bad*, we are always putting that on the children, and then we beat them into submission psychologically. I know that is a harsh way of putting it, and yet that is what we do to their minds when we tell them to be a *good boy* or a *good girl*. We were all beaten into submission to make sure we fit the definition of *good child*, a *smart child* or be whatever society said we needed to be. We teach our children based on how we were treated even if we think we are doing it differently than our parents.

We teach them based on the rules we learned. We have been forced into a linear way of thinking, and a linear way of thinking says *boy* or *girl*; then it becomes a *good boy* or a *good girl*. We are putting our thoughts on the child from the minute they are born. We start the illusion of labels, and we teach them from those illusions. Then somewhere down the line, we no longer have just a *man*; we have to have a *real man*. Next we have to have a *real good man* or a *real bad man*, which started with a child being a *good boy* or a *bad boy*. Very quickly people get weighted down and cannot live their lives. They are living the labels.

Unfortunately, a child will absorb all the illusions in the first few years, probably by the age of four. Children create their whole lives from those first critical years. All the things they were taught and the manner in which they were taught is what they will use to create their lives. Around the age of four years children die psychologically, and they become robots—programmed, repetitious entities. The same happened to each of us around the same age. So, just realize that you and all of us died to our real selves at a very young age; and as you raise your child, you will realize that you are also raising yourself. Right now, our behavior on this planet portrays us all as angry children.

Knowing Nothing

If you think you already know something about raising a child, you might as well not read what is presented here because in order to raise a sane/transformed child, you will have to start from zero. To do things in a new way, not the way you have been taught, you need to start from zero. In order to start from zero, you must see that you don't know anything. If you think you know something, you are not at zero. What is presented here is much like the "… For Dummies" books where you see that in one domain you don't know anything. That is starting from zero. In seeing that, you have the most to gain.

What I am speaking about here is *new*, meaning never having been before on planet earth. So if you say that you don't know what to do to raise a child; but in the back of your mind you have some places where you think you do know, then that is not 100 percent not knowing. Admitting you don't know and seeing it totally in all areas of your life without missing one place is 100 percent. Seeing something 100 percent would cause a transformation in you.

Humility is admitting you don't know what to do to raise a child. Notice I didn't say *how* because *how* sends you off to the books to read how. If someone is writing a book on how to raise a child, they are writing it based on their already existing knowledge which is flawed.

I didn't know how to approach the topic of raising a child as a transformed being because the only way to raise a child is to raise it in *the now*, in the moment of the happening, and to realize that to raise a child perfectly you have to realize you don't know how to do it and admit you don't know how to do it. That is humility.

It would be a big benefit to say "I don't know how to raise a child," and go on from there and admit that you don't know how to live on this insane planet. It is almost like saying "the greater the level of humility the greater the person you are." That sounds a little strange, doesn't it? Yet, that is what happens.

For most people the definition of humility is to not be egotistical. But humility really means that you *don't know* and admit it. Humility is seeing in each instant that you don't know. If you go around just repeating that you don't know and not really seeing it 100 percent, that would be just repeating words without meaning. The mind likes to trick us and the smarter the mind, the more it knows how to trick us. We might say that we don't know what is needed to raise a sane child and yet have an idea of some parts of parenting. So it is not a 100 percent "I do not know." This might be all you can do for now, so keep doing it and watching yourself. Watch the thoughts that arise and notice if it is a mind trick or a true "I don't know."

It is difficult for most people to admit that they don't know, and knowing nothing is part of being humble or having humility. That is the place discovery happens. Colleges and schools and churches are where learning happens. Discovery and learning are two different things.

Humility is to accept that the child has intelligence and the parents have lost it. That is very frightening for many people. It is almost like admitting their whole life has been worthless, useless, wrong, etc. It is almost like dying psychologically, and dying is needed in order to start anew, in order to raise a sane child. Seeing that you don't know would bring an end to everything you think you know about raising a child. Not knowing allows for something new to show up. Unless something comes from what is *not* already known, it is not intelligence because all that we know is of our past and all of that has failed. Technologically, we have made tremendous strides, but psychologically we are just as ignorant as we were thousands of years ago. We are still jealous, angry, prideful, believing in gods, having superstitions, fighting, maiming and murdering.

For thousands of years we have been dragging around what we already know into the next generation, hoping that will somehow bring peace on earth; but every child is introduced into a violent world that goes to war, and they grow up and go to war because that is what they are taught. We are continuing war with each generation.

In the way we currently interact with our children, the more intelligence is crushed out of them. With a partnership there is possibility of acknowledging the child as being the intelligent one and to look to the child as your teacher or guide. A partnership is formed when each person is equal. If someone were to ask you who is your teacher to assist with raising the child and you were to answer that it is the child, you would probably be ridiculed. To discover what a child needs and what a child knows, you would have to give up everything you think you know about what a child needs and just be there with the child and respond accordingly at that moment.

Many people might offhandedly admit that they don't know how to be a parent, but they probably wouldn't really mean it. They think in some areas they do know. They had parents, so they have an idea of what parenting is. Yet, when it comes to being a partner, there is a real unknown there. They are in the domain of not knowing what that is, and that is where they need to be. That is discovery. Intelligence is in what you don't know.

Transformation Ends Conditioning

Transformation is the most important thing that could happen in today's world because transformation is the ending of the program we created for ourselves. To end the repetition of programming, we need to begin simply by letting go of the labels, starting with son, daughter, mother or father. Also, we need to let go of adding an ownership, including the word *our*, like *our son* or *our daughter*. Anything we own ends up owing us. Ownership is a trap we fall into, both the adult and the child.

Instead we need to create a partnership between the child and the adult. The adults would need to see that up until the child is age four, the child is 99 percent more intelligent than the adult. This is a difficult thing to see because the parents think they are the smart ones, which is true, but their smart is based on all the knowledge they have accumulated. A child has a huge open space of intelligence, creation and love that it is born with, and the child is that intelligence, creation and love.

The difference between knowledge and intelligence is that knowledge comes from learning through books and stories we remember told by others, whereas intelligence comes from the unknown. You could call intelligence *awareness* not based on what we already know.

We care to have our children able to function in society, and in order to do that we train them, and we think that training is needed so that children will be accepted and not have sad lives. We want our children to be happy, and we think what we teach them will give it to them. We think we are doing the right thing when in actuality we are doing the most destructive thing. We are doing what will cause the thing we don't want—sadness, rejection, etc. We are molding the children to fit into an insane society. We are

8

saying to them that unless you grow up insane, you are not going to fit in.

The difficulty is that the parents must first look and see that they are totally conditioned and insane and that there is a possibility for transformation. Transformation is the death of everything we have been taught. With that death we can begin to use intelligence rather that knowledge to bring up children. However, we do not have the contextual consideration that we ourselves are insane.

The greatest possibility of bringing up a sane, transformed child is to explain to the child when we can that we ourselves are crazy, not whole, but we would like to be in a partnership with the child to see if that can end the insanity. Although by the time we can have this actual conversation and have it heard, the child will already be conditioned into insanity. It is difficult to say if an insane person could bring forth a sane child. It would almost have to be that the parents themselves are transformed and enlightened beings.

Right now, the only real possibility of bringing up children who are whole, healthy and able to grow up to take care of themselves is for them to do it. It is possible for the parents to make enough mistakes that children come out with a balanced outlook on life. It would be the manner in which parents raise a child with all the mistakes they make that does it. It won't be the stuff they think they are doing right. It would be the little tiny things they don't do.

If I were sending a child to school, I would tell the child that we are about to go to one of the craziest places ever. They are not going to do anything to assist in creating any intelligence for you, but you do need to learn to read, write and do arithmetic. So get those things from school, and do your best not to let the rest of it affect you too much. My guess would be that the child will have A's all the way through school because he wouldn't be trying. There is no such thing as trying. You either do or you don't do. You either fail or you succeed.

Children's Sensitivity

Parents don't realize the child is ninety-nine percent more sensitive than they are. The smallest thing is a big thing for children. Children are so enlivened and sensitive to the world around them that they notice everything. Small things like a little pain or their intestinal functions are extreme. For instance, if they have to burp and cannot, they feel like they are almost going to die. They don't have any rational thought about it. They are extremely aware of every body function, and that is how they assimilate things. Adults don't realize this and don't have compassion for the sensitivity the child has. We are not aware of the sensitivity they have, and even the tone of our voice and everything about the manner in which we are around them is directly transferred to the child. Since most adults were desensitized by their upbringing by desensitized parents, they cannot see how sensitive children are. Parents just aren't aware of what they are doing and how that will affect the child.

When children become ill, they have a far greater possibility of having a partnership in the moment with their parents. If a child is colicky or has other problems, the parents need to give more attention, be more in the moment and listen with the child to its needs. Unfortunately, these days there is a trend to take the child to the doctor and have the child be given drugs, thinking that this is what a good mother does, so even that possibility for partnership has been taken away.

If parents would create a partnership with the child, there is the possibility that the child could facilitate a transformation of the parents. From the minute a child is born, say to the child "you are my partner."

Yes, go outside the hospital and say "I have a new partner in my life. Right now this child is only a few hours old, and together we will see what this world is all about."

Naming children is their first label, and it is necessary because there are seven billion of us, so there is that need for differentiation. And you might be surprised to know that people even create a little bit of pride around their names. People have a connection, if you will, to their names, but the name itself is only necessary for the differentiation between people.

Other than just being ourselves, the closest we get to reality is the name we were given at our birth. That is one reason the men of history have made women change their names in marriage. The men didn't want to take the chance that the women would discover themselves later on in life. They wanted them to be subservient, pregnant and owned. To begin with, it is a huge challenge to discover who you are while you are the same name you were born with; but if you were born Smith and then changed it to Guggenheim, that actually adds to the confusion. The more labels that are added, such as *Mrs.*, *wife*, *mother*, as well as adding *my wife* to it, the greater the confusion.

Dysfunctional is the normal of our present manner of living on this planet, so it would be a huge possibility for people's transformation to realize that they are dysfunctional parents. Before they even start off, they are dysfunctional parents; and no matter what they think of their parents, they are the offspring of dysfunctional parents, who were the offspring of dysfunctional parents— going back a few thousand years of conditioning. Of course, many people will say they had dysfunctional parents, but they think they will be better than their parents were, and that they'll do it differently. That almost guarantees they will be the same even though they think they are different.

Opposites are always the same only we don't see it. They are both beliefs. You might say that you are not going to spank your child, and that you will never yell at them; so you don't spank your child, but you put the child in the corner or use manipulation. Which is worse? Either action sends a negative connotation to the child.

I would guess that most parents want their children to be happy, and there is dilemma to that. We say when our children are born that all we want is for them to be happy, not realizing that happy is half of sad. *Happy* is causing a child to be dualistic in the world of opposites, such as good/bad, happy/sad, right/wrong. We don't realize that when we want one thing, the negative side is being created as well, and the negative side is what our planet is stuck in. It has a tiny spectrum of positive in it, but for the most part we are negative.

We Live in a Violent World

We go to war, we kill each other, we fight with each other, and we get angry. If you ask people what they think of an entity that kills itself, they would probably answer that would be horrible! Yet we don't see that is what we are doing. We don't think that killing people of another nation or someone we have created as an enemy is the same as killing ourselves. We name it war and that makes it justified.

The more wars, the more violence and the more fights we have, the greater our birth rate is going to be. The fewer of those things we have, the less the birth rate will be because it is the violence and the killing and the fear of loss that causes the birth rate to go up. We fear losing our lineage and losing the possibility of humans to continue when in truth we are losing that. In years past people had large families to help on the farm or range, and all of that is part of the conditioning from our past. We are losing the possibility of the continuation of the human species on our present path.

Of course, there is a biological drive for the procreation of the species, and to that natural drive we add the beliefs we were taught as children. When we are very young, we are asked how many children we are going to have when we get married. We are given the plan to follow— graduate high school, go to college, get a good job, get married, have children, retire and die.

If you ever look around at the enlightened gurus and transformed entities, you will notice that most do not have children, mostly because of the condition of our world. They see all the pain and suffering that is here, and they realize they would not want to bring forth another human being to be in pain and suffering. I asked my son when he was 12 years of age if he would want to bring another human being into this world of killing, violence and suffering. He replied with a resounding "no," and to this day he has not.

One of the most difficult things for a person to realize is that the greater the level of success they have, the larger the level of insanity they actually live in. So the greatest failures, the ones we think of as successes, are the presidents, the CEOs, all the rich and famous people. Those people are the greatest disasters, for they are the ones who have the money that keeps our world going the way it is. Most everyone else strives to be these people, the *power people*, so they look at that as their goal. These powerful people keep things as they are—in the state of violence. They are throwing money at solutions instead of solving the problems.

A perfect Pope would stand up on the pulpit and say, "From this day forward we are going to put ourselves out of business. We will give away all our belongings and all our money and our food and no longer preach about these things because we will be too busy doing them."

That is the difference between what *love* is and what *in love* is, as well as the difference between what intelligence is and what knowledge is. Love and intelligence are the doing of it. Knowledge and *in love,* which come from beliefs and thoughts, are the explanations of it, the talking of it and the plans and the goals.

Currently we do not have love on this planet. We only have *in love*. We have the belief of love, not the actuality of it. If we did love our children, we wouldn't train and condition them as we were trained and conditioned. We would prepare the planet for the children; not prepare the children for the planet.

Forming a Partnership

A child's actions would determine the parent's actions. The consequences or results would be there for the child no matter what. And if the world blocked the consequences, the parent would need to provide the consequences even if it had to be somewhat of a fake consequence. Intelligence and love would dictate what that would be in the moment, in the action of the happening.

Being in the moment with each other happens in many cases with a new born child and the new mother. In the moment a child is born, there are two perfect entities—the mother and the child. They are perfect, for they have both just been born, so to speak. From then on the division begins. From there it is the mother exerting her will on the child in the belief that she is right and she is teaching the child.

Transformed parents would use all their energy to discover all they could learn from the child from the moment of birth. Conversely, the normal, non-transformed parent finds out what they can teach the child, or they think they already know how to mold the child. The transformed parent would have the child mold the parent, at least when it comes to the child itself, and that would never stop. There would always be that partnership. A partnership means when there is a mistake made, it is made by two people if it is a two person partnership. If we always had in mind that when the child makes a mistake it would be our mistake as well, a partnership would be created. The one thing we wouldn't need to do is blame the child. That is the biggest mistake we make. We do things like smack their hands, or we yell at them, or we say "don't do that." We put them down and we make them wrong.

Our world is made up of *right* and *wrong* and *good* and *bad*. Everything is dualistic, having an opposite, and making a mistake is *bad*. Mistakes happen a lot of the time. They are not something to be ashamed of; and in a partnership, we would all take responsibility for any mistake that happens. If we start out with a partnership, i.e., walking together the whole time, then it would be an almost natural act that every part of what a child does or every mistake he or she makes is a collective mistake, no matter if the child takes responsibility for it or not. I am not talking about *blame* when I say *responsibility*. Responsibility is realizing or seeing that we created the happening without any judgment or opinion added to it. *Blame* is when we make the other person wrong and we have a feeling or judgment about it.

Truth spoken is where the rubber hits the road. All of the gurus and all of the books can talk about these things, but when does it become real? It becomes real when we hold that child in our hands and we speak with it and say, "We are partners," and we actually do it—partners in truth; partners in life.

Until there is *Heaven on Earth*, which is essentially what I am speaking of, there is only confusion. There is only insanity. I said before that the child is 99 percent more intelligent than the parent, yet who is responsible for the upbringing of the child? It is insane parents when actually the child should be in charge, if there were such a thing as *in charge*. That is the thing about a partnership. There is no one in charge.

In order to improve being a mother or father you need to stop being a mother or a father. End being the programmed robot that was taught what mothers, fathers or parents do or what they are, such as *good* or *bad* mother or father.

When you create a partnership with children, it allows them to be who they are and the parents to be who they are. In a partnership there is a discussion when something comes up—a discussion without any anger, accusations or blame. Make an agreement with each other that you can say whatever you see and they can say whatever they see and then have a discussion about it without anger or judgment.

Consequences vs. Punishment

When we talk about the dynamics of bringing up a sane child in an insane world and the things to do which cannot be done, we cannot, as in the past, get into rules about things. For example, we once had rules that if the children were bad, we put them in the corner or made them wear dunce caps and all sorts of insane things. I am speaking of walking with them in the moment; therefore, no rules could be made ahead of time. Rules make it easy because then we don't have to be in the moment with the child. We just go to the rule book and look up the answer, or we act from what our parents did.

There is a need for consequences, and natural consequences usually happen. For example, if the child gets too close to fire, they feel the heat and pull away before they get burned, thus learning about fire. However, our planet blocks the consequences. We are afraid the child will get burned if they go too close to a fire, so we stop the discovery resulting in their natural intelligence being stifled.

If we are in a partnership, we do things together hand in hand, so to speak. If a child makes a mess, we both clean it together or play with it together, and we don't make the child wrong. We just say that we made a mess, so what are we going to do? Then be in the moment to clean it or play with it or leave it. There is no right or wrong answer here. In living our lives, there can be no rules, except that we need rules to live our life. When does a rule get in the way? It is when it is firm, rigid and a belief.

If we continue to work together with the child, at some point the child might do some action such as deliberately spilling milk in order to get attention. Again, that is not bad. It is part of their experimenting with their environment. Yet, you would not want to reward that activity by cleaning up the milk yourself, for that will shift what you are doing here. You would have the child clean it up. If you clean it up yourself, you are teaching children they are not responsible for their actions; therefore, they would do it again.

The distinction between punishment and consequences is that consequences happen because of an action which comes naturally whereas a punishment happens when we think we are right or think something or someone else is wrong. There is no escaping consequence even though a consequence isn't often immediate or seen as the result of an action taken. For children, if there isn't a natural consequence that happens immediately after the event, then often a consequence needs to be manufactured by the parent if you weren't there when it happened, or you were there but it wasn't appropriate to deal with it at that time. This is not done to prove right or wrong. It is done to allow children to see that their actions have consequences. You say to the child that this is a consequence of your action, without using the word *punishment*.

It is important for the child to have these consequences. Today's parents want to blame the school or blame another child if their child gets into trouble, and they stand up for their child. This is a detriment to the child, as the child learns they can get away with things and you will take care of it. Then the child will do more and more things to test the limits and often feel proud of getting away with it. They also will continue doing it because they get attention. When else do parents stand up for their children? It is not often, not unless the child is in trouble. Children like it when their parents stand up for them. What will children do to have you stand up for them? They will keep doing what you consider *bad* things.

Part of the lesson with consequences is learning to take responsibility, to learn that we all make mistakes, to learn that mistakes have consequences and not be afraid of them or try to avoid them. The consequences are not to be done in anger or with any tone in your voice other than care and concern for the child. It is always best if the consequences are in the moment of the event, yet that isn't always possible. In either case, if you are the one administering the consequences, it needs to be done with no animosity, revenge or anger. Something that happened on its own, such as touching a hot iron has immediate consequences and nothing is needed from you other than checking to see if the hand is OK.

Before you start to speak, ask yourself if you are upset about what the child did. If so, deal with your own feelings before talking with the child, especially before you give any consequences. Often parents come out with a ridiculous consequence they regret because they realize it was not reasonable. Often you take it back and then don't give the child another. Again the child is getting away with something. Speak with them when you can be calm and after you have dealt with your issues regarding the event. Partnership means you don't take power over the child and vice versa. You both work together with caring for each other. It is a tricky thing to do as we are all in our own world, not realizing what we are doing either to ourselves or to others.

Sometimes the child might be in trouble at school because he didn't follow a rule that you think is a silly rule, so you don't feel he needs consequences. It is still important to teach children to live in a society and to know that there will be consequences when the rules are broken even if you don't agree with the rules. Talk with the child with a clear mind, with no anger or feelings attached.

Parents with a clear mind would be aware that there is no *good* or *bad* or a *right* and *wrong* and would explain that to the child. Also, point out to the child that he knew there was a rule, and he needed to follow it.

A child's actions might have been innocent, and yet they still need to learn, with care and concern, that people make mistakes and that there are consequences. Since our society is full of rules, and at this time rules are needed, it is important to talk with the child and let him know there is a time and place for everything. I cannot say it enough that all this needs to be done while the parent is not angry or sad or has any other feelings attached because then the message will come through as a punishment that the child did something wrong, which teaches violence, not caring.

All of this comes back to parents having clarity of mind and speaking with the child from a partnership. Clarity of mind cannot *want*, clarity of mind cannot have the need for *more,* and clarity of mind would not have a goal for the child. Parents would have the consideration that the child just be a child and watch what happens. Be a partner in their growth. Clarity of mind erases your history—your conditioned past. It doesn't erase the memories. It erases the attachments to those memories. It erases all the things we have added to our lives—the illusions and beliefs we were taught and accepted.

Breaking Patterns

In being with each situation as it arises, you could do each one differently than you usually would. This will break the habit of repetition. To do something differently, even something as mundane as loading the dishwasher, experiment with doing it differently every day. It drives the mind crazy to break apart a rule. The mind wants to do things the same way all the time just like a robot, so we fall asleep and let the robot run our lives.

The same thing is true in raising a child. The minute we see the child has caught onto a pattern, a repetitive action, it needs to be broken; therefore, we need to do something differently. Currently, we like to see our children repeat a pattern because we think it means they are learning things. We teach them to repeat. This is the beginning of their training to become a conditioned robot. As soon as you see a pattern forming, break it and do it anew. Do it differently. That is showing your children how to live their lives in the moment rather than repeating something they are conditioned to do.

All that I speak of here has to do with the parents' lives and the way they live them. Let's say that one of the parents has had a death or transformational experience and the other one hasn't. Some disagreements will probably arise in the way things are done. One cares to do things differently while the one who hadn't had the experience would more likely think that was a strange or wrong way of doing it. So then there is tension between the two since both have an idea of what should be happening in that instance. Ninety-nine percent of the time, the transformed being is going to just let up because intelligence cannot fight, it cannot argue and it cannot use force in order to get an action. That is why our world is completely encased in violence right now—there is no intelligence.

If you are the parent of a child of any age and care to have one contextual action in which to discover yourself, it could be in this thing called *child rearing*. That would be a perfect place to start. If we truly discover we don't know what to do to raise a child, we probably would also instantly see that we didn't know how to raise ourselves. Our parents raised us in conjunction with our world and all that is in it— church and school and all the rules we were taught. Yet, it was up to each one of us to accept these things; and upon accepting them; we were the ones raising ourselves. For example, the first time we learned about lies was when we were told not to lie.

This whole contextual action I care to happen for those listening with me is a discovery of "I don't know" which is something like discovering the space between two thoughts. First, we need to discover that there is a space between two thoughts because most people don't realize that. People have continuous thoughts going on, sometimes multiple thoughts at the same time. So if we realize there is a space between two thoughts and catch that spot, it's going to be tiny. But as in raising a child, if we see we don't know what to do to raise a child, we can begin expanding the discovery of what to do to raise a child. If we discover the space between two thoughts, we can begin to expand that as well. If we get it to a certain spot we will discover, if we are alive and aware, that not only we didn't know what to do to raise a child, we didn't know what to do to raise ourselves.

Because we didn't know what to do to raise ourselves, we let our parents and the world raise us. So, now new moms and dads don't know what to do to raise a child, and they are raising the child. Still they think they know what to do because they learned from their parents. We are raising our children the same way we were raised. Even if we think we are raising them the opposite of how our parents did, it's still the same way because all opposites, like *right/wrong, good/bad, sad/happy,* are the same dualistic action. It is only when both *right and wrong* are right and both *right and wrong* are wrong that we begin to have some sort of a new beginning or opening.

Seeing vs. Knowing

The context of what I speak has to do with the birth of intelligence. So we have to go back now and ask "are you intelligent?" You might then ask what intelligence is, or you might realize it can't be described, or your mind might trick you into thinking you are intelligent. To say you don't know is a direct assault on the ego because nobody cares to admit that, yet the secret to life is humility which means you don't know. All *knowing* is of knowledge, and *seeing* is of intelligence. *Seeing* is in the action of *the now*. It is seeing what is real.

Perhaps this is where it gets a bit sticky because if we see in *the now* that we don't know anything; and then we come to the next *now* and say we don't know anything, can it be the same now? If we are going to say it again, where do we have to say it from? We have to say it from a new place which would also include the seeing of it in *the now*, not just the repetition and not just saying that yesterday "I didn't know anything and today I don't know anything." In the instant without any feelings or attachments, say "I don't know anything." So here it is 8:01 A.M. and you're seeing you don't know anything. Then here it is 8:02 A.M., and you're seeing you don't know anything. Now where did both of those come from? They came from personal observation, didn't they? They came from *the now,* the observation in the instant of awareness by saying "I don't know."

I am speaking psychologically of *not knowing*, but even with the things we were taught, we don't know for sure if they're right. We accept a general agreement which makes us believe something is right. *Knowing* is accepting something that has already been established as a fact which is often confused with what is true or the truth. If you accept what has already been established and already been lived, what are you living? You are living your history. We could be, and have been, called *the walking dead*. We are dragging everything that has gone before and bringing it into *the now*, so actually there is no *now* when we do that.

All of this has to do with being free, free to be the stupidest person that has ever lived and free to be the most intelligent being that ever bloomed on this planet. Free to be anything. Free to be you. There is no sadness or pride or feeling or judgment of any kind with either of those statements. They both mean the same thing. So where is the pain and suffering in either of those statements or any statement spoken? If you are free, you don't have any feelings about them because you don't see those statements as different. There are no feelings attached to either one. There is neither offense nor defense taken. It means you remove 100 percent of the criticisms and 100 percent of the complements.

Much of what I am saying is ethereal, as it has never been. We cannot go into the task of raising a child already knowing what to do to raise a child because all we will bring forth is everything that we have already had on this planet. We might begin, however, by showing the child that there is no right or wrong; good or bad and, most importantly, no competition.

Competition is teaching to glorify the right/wrong or winner/loser. Competition includes being the most right. So if we took a world of children that didn't have a right/wrong or good/bad and didn't have competition, what kind of world would we have? We would have a world where everyone is equal. Yet, people argue that if we didn't have competition, we wouldn't strive for things or that we wouldn't have had any of the great achievements we have had. But that is not true because the actual intelligence or energy to do those things comes before the competition. Competition is also teaching a form of violence as it is pitting one person against another.

We haven't discovered the depths of our oceans or our earth, and we are floating around in space trying to take our insanity somewhere else. We here on planet earth have not even discovered ourselves. How stupid was it for a country to fly to the moon and stick a flag on it? Is an alien going to come by and see that the moon was already claimed by someone else and move on? That is the epitome of ownership, competition and pride. We are saying, "Look what we did. We beat you in the race to the moon. We are better and smarter than you."

The Gift of Failure

Up until this point we have been talking about bringing forth children who were just born, that are new. What if we have children who are already grown and screwed up? What is it we can do now at this point?

One of the things we are taught is that if children grow up to be doctors, lawyers and executives, they are the successful ones; and the ones who are thieves, liars or cheats are the unsuccessful ones. So what does a parent do if they have either of these children or anything in-between? The answer for either one is the same. It is to say "I have failed" because if a child grows up to be a success in an already insane world, what does that indicate? It indicates they are insane. And if the child grows to be unsuccessful based on societal values, that person is equally a failure. They usually have to be taken care of by others and cannot make it on their own.

Our world is set up for always striving for success, and that success is measured by the amount of money we have. That is a big part of what is causing the insanity of this world—always striving for monetary success. To be successful in an insane world would mean the more successful you are the more insane you are. That is usually true. The ones holding all the money are the ones most insane, the ones keeping the insanity alive.

If people could see there is greater possibility in failure than success, they wouldn't be trying so hard to succeed. That is where I had my opening to transformation, in the seeing of my failures. I saw them completely, and in that seeing, I saw the infinite possibilities that were there for me. Seeing my failures opened up a whole new world of sanity.

What is the common denominator for all mothers and fathers? We have all failed. Now here is a secret. When you see that you are a failure, you are given a gift that creates an opening, a space. That space clears it all so that you can begin anew. It clears it for the female, the mother, and the male, the father, to raise themselves so that they can raise the child. Even if the child is older, most parents will still be raising that child. Even if you don't have much communication between each other, that bond is still there. What would happen if your offspring came back and you were different, completely new? There might be some confusion and possibly even some frustration or even anger because your offspring want you to stay the same so they can stay the same. As much as people say they want things to change, they don't want to be the ones who change.

So, the important thing for parents to do, no matter what the age of the child, is to see that they failed. And the failure was that they accepted the way their parents raised them. There is a dual thing that happens almost simultaneously. Our parents screwed up our minds totally, and instantaneously we did it too. We did it because we accepted our conditioning. Now this might be very difficult to see as it throws blame out the window, but it does leave one thing—responsibility. Blame creates justifications and excuses. "My dad beat me, so I beat my kids," or "my mom drank until she passed out, and I turned out OK." We might say that we had the greatest parents in the world or we had the worst parents in the world. It doesn't matter. All of that is the same. The only thing that has any impact is responsibility.

You need to realize you are raising a child, and that child is you. As you begin raising yourself, you will see you. You might look at what you did, and then look at what your children are doing because they are perfect mirrors. All you have to do is look at them and see the things you did and the things you made them do. You might be either proud of it or ashamed of it, but whatever they are doing and being, it is all the same.

Breaking the Chains

So, what's the secret to ending all of this failure? You break the chains, the chains of the past you are carrying around with you. Break every one you discover in the instance of the discovery. When you, for yourself, begin to show up new, the past goes as well. The old manipulations from all sides, yours, as well as your children's and as well as your parents', will all be gone.

So what must the others do then when you are different? At first they might want to find a new manipulation, a new way of getting what they are used to getting and then create a new chain. The old manipulations were difficult or even impossible for you to see because you were so used to them, and everyone was playing the same game—"I manipulate you to get what I want, and you manipulate me to get what you want." But if you remove the manipulation, the chain, they will have to find a new way to get what they want, and that will be very easy for you to see because it will be new. Once you break a chain, it goes in all directions. It goes from you to your children and from you to your parents as well.

The chains are not just connected to our children and our parents. These chains connect us to many, possibly to everyone on the planet as we are all interconnected, and we are interconnected to a violent consciousness. They are the chains that hold us to the past, to the conditioning of our planet, to all the suffering and violence. I say to cut all of the chains and connections each of us comes across. That would mean we would be entirely alone, which we already are.

If there is to be a perfect world, then each of us needs to be perfect within ourselves, and that is done by shattering the chains. That is what we are breaking, and the vehicle we are using to break those chains is the question, "Can we raise a sane/transformed child?" The child is actually you. We do not need to bring forth a child to see this since the child you are raising is yourself. You brought forth a child and it was you, and you failed at raising that child. Then you had children and continued that failure.

By the time each child reaches an age of around four, that child is already what I call a *conditioned robot.* By that age, children just repeat without questioning the training they were taught. We are all stuck at that point in our development. Between the ages of zero and four we freeze ourselves psychologically. We accept the insanity of our parents. We are all children of around four years of age even though our bodies continue to grow, and we continue to get older. We get married and have children, but psychologically we are all still four-years old. If you look around, you will see that is true. All the killing and violence on earth is like four-year olds having a tantrum, fighting over their toys. Where else would we see religions that promote peace on earth and yet ask people to go out and kill for that cause? We don't see the hypocrisy in it or the insanity of it.

In raising a child, the first thing to see is that you are the child. You had one chance to raise that child, and you failed. We all failed, and we will continue to fail unless we speak the truth of it. Saying that you had one chance with one child, yourself, and you failed opens the possibility of something new, but first you have to get to the place where you can see you are still a child.

Raising Your Inner Child

Some people do a practice they call *inner child* work in which they go back in time and comfort that part of them that was frozen in time due to a trauma. What I am talking about is something different. I say that the most fantastic, miraculous place to meet your inner child is while you are cooking eggs, while you are making love to your partner, while you are fighting with another person, while you are in your life and while you are in *the now* because that is where your inner child is. It shows up in the *now*, not in the past.

There are a few large problems with doing the first mentioned kind of inner child work. One is that you are using your memory to remember something that happened many years ago, and memory is faulty. We think we remember things with all the correct details, yet most people cannot remember something that happened yesterday, let alone many years ago. We have attached many feelings to a situation, so it is already a lie. Attachments are judgments and opinions, and anything that has any feeling or attachment is no longer true.

When you go into the past as those processes do, it is to find a hurt, a trauma and a drama. It promotes being a victim, meaning you had been abused in some way, and it is a victim who goes on to abuse others. The people who abuse others think they are a victim of something that justifies in their mind the acts they are doing. Many abusers think they are actually just defending themselves with the actions they take.

The feeling of being a victim causes an abuser. When people feel like they need to defend themselves, they go out and buy a gun to shoot someone. By the very nature of the fact that they are willing to shoot someone, what are they saying? They are saying that their life is more important than anyone else's, and that is the beginning of World War III. It will always come down to that. The moment we put ourselves above another person, World War III has begun, and at that moment we are really killing ourselves.

I say that you can see that inner child in every moment of your life as you are living your life. See how you are being that child in the way you are acting or, more likely, reacting to what is going on. See that you are that little four-year old having a tantrum when you don't get what you want. See you as that little girl or little boy getting your feelings hurt when someone says something that offends you. Watch and see as that child is still very active and running your life.

Creating intent to raise a sane child focuses our energy in that one area. We then take our abilities and focus them on the intent to raise a sane child, and who is the child? *You* are that child. That takes you to a whole new domain of activity, a whole new way of being. But currently we cannot raise a child ourselves because we are still children. Now you will see that it is not another child we are speaking of. It is you who is still a child, so the question is: Can you raise yourself? See that you are still a child, stuck and frozen in time at the age of around four. See that you failed at raising a child—you. Focus doesn't mean to narrow down your seeing and looking. It means to have a contextual action called *is it possible to raise a sane child;* then look at what shows up. Look at your life in the moment as it is happening, in *the now*. This is difficult because it is very empowering.

The World's Worst

If I were to say to you that you are the dumbest person on this planet, there would probably be a reaction of anger on your part. On the other hand, you may experience that on your own, by yourself, without any feelings attached to it.

You might say that you failed and so has every other mother and father. Adding other people when you say that dilutes your seeing of it. Misery loves company, so you bring in everyone else. It justifies you not taking 100 percent responsibility and excuses it. "Everyone else does it, so it is OK for me to do it, too." If you say that you failed and look at yourself only with the fact that you failed, where does that bring the impact? It brings it to you.

Humility is created when you see your failures and speak them. The greater the humility, if there were a greater, the greater your spring forward in the other direction would be. If you say that you have been *kind of bad*, you might move forward a little bit. How about if you say you are the *world's worst*? Then the greater the movement would be. In a physical domain, you can equate this to shooting an arrow. The further back you pull the bow string, the further the arrow flies. This is all for an example as a way of explaining failure so you can follow what I am saying. So in quantum, like magic, you would go from being the *worst person* in the world to being the *best person* who walked the planet. If you really see this, that is how the movement would be—in quantum. Of course, you would have to really *see* it for this movement to happen. So, if you don't notice the movement, you haven't seen what I am talking about fully, 100 percent.

I am not suggesting that you keep repeating over and over "I am a failure," or "I am the worst person in the world" because that would just be repeating from the mind. I am speaking of seeing it through the discovery of it, through the living it and seeing it in the moment of it happening. That will cause the shift to transformation.

If you care to see that—the dumbest, the worst, the failure, etc.—then question and watch to see what comes up. Say to yourself, "If I am the dumbest, the worst and a failure, let me see what I do." Then watch your life and notice the things you do and the things you think. Notice yourself in your relationships with your children and all others in the world. Each time you say any of that, speak it anew, not in a way of just repeating it as in affirmations, but an actual looking at it each time you speak it.

Speaking is the act of creation. When you say something one time, and it is the first time you say it, that *something* is created. If you repeat it, it is invented, and invention is where we are stuck—in repeating the past. So each time you say something, say it anew and look at it anew. If you look and see that you are failing, seeing that you are dumb or whatever, you are noticing anew each time you are that.

Developing Images

When we begin a relationship, we begin to develop an image of the other person, and then we expect that person to stay that way. So in essence, we freeze that person in our minds even if the other makes some adjustment. What would be a way to not have this pre-defined image of your partner? Wouldn't it be to *not* have those expectations that keep others frozen as they are? Looking at your partner without already knowing him or her is huge for relationships. Check the ones in your life anew and look at them anew every day or every moment. Check to see if they are the same or if you are the same, i.e., holding the same image of them. Don't assume they will be this way or that way. Really look at them and yourself, and check your thinking each time. Do not attempt to drop your image because that is almost impossible and often enhances an image. In order to check it, you could ask the question, "If in the past this person was like . . ., are they like that now?" Then look at it anew. Are they the same, or are they the same because you are making them that way?

We keep people the same by acting in the manner we act to make sure they stay the same. We are all caught up in repeating patterns, and we are all doing it to each other by keeping each other the same as we think them to be. I am not suggesting a person isn't the way they are, yet I am suggesting that their partner might be keeping them that way and vice versa. We all do it. We have a pre-defined image, and then we don't check to see if others are still the same. Check to see their actions and check to see your reactions.

My suggestion for our planet and for the raising of children, starting with us, is for each of us to realize that we screwed up in raising ourselves and start there. Then our planet will look brand-spanking new. We cause our children to be the way they are, and it doesn't matter if we complain about them or complement them. Both actions are the same.

Earlier we were speaking of breaking the chains that keep us all stuck in the same repeating pattern. Now, if we break the chain, in what direction will it go? Have you ever played tug of war? If the rope breaks, the players snap away from each other. The same is true with the chain. It goes in both directions. It breaks the chains that keep you tied to your children and to your parents, and then there will be a bit of a shock. You will see that you are alone, which is your worst fear and your greatest opportunity to discover who you are. When you look inside of you, you will see *only* you. No one else is there.

The Action of Creation

The creation I speak of is not creation and then destruction. Destruction implies a violent action. The creation I speak of comes when there is an ending. The word *ending* is much softer. It is a melting down to nothing. The only way something new can be brought forth is for the old to end. In the psychological that would imply a natural ending—bringing what is there to an end. That is the only way creation can be. Everything else is invention. Invention is taking what we already have and making something else out of it.

Creation is having nothing and bringing forth something. So when there is already something there, it needs to end. The ending would then leave a blank space. There needs to be that blank space for creation to happen. It isn't dualistic in manner as is the destruction/creation we are now living. I am speaking of an ending and a beginning that occurs naturally. When something has an opposite, it is duality. It is fake because it is of thought. It is not real.

There is creation, for which I am responsible. Then there is intelligence; then there is love; and then there is truth. Something is created from nothing, and I am responsible for that. Then there is intelligence which holds what has been created. Next there is love which delivers the creation onto the planet, and then there is truth which is the speaking of it without thinking it is true. We could say that truth is half real and half not real. The entryway to truth is to speak the truth. Speaking requires thinking, and when once spoken through thought, it is no longer true. If you hold onto the truth, it becomes a belief.

People talk of love, yet as love is defined currently on this planet it comes with hate, the opposite. If we allow that *love* is simply action, then it doesn't have any judgment or opinion or opposite with it. There would be no "I love this," and no "I hate that," or even "I love my husband." Love is action. Love is life force energy. We cannot find it because we don't know what it is. So what does that leave when you ask what is love or what do you love? You might say that you love your child, and then look at the manner in which your child turned out, developed and grew. If you could really see this world, would you say that someone who really loved children would bring them into such an insane world, a world full of suffering and pain and misery?

Although many people will not admit it, having children is more of a conditioning and a *want* than love. We are brought up being told and conditioned to want children. Those people who cannot or choose to not have children often feel *less than* and shunned because of it.

This thing called love, I say, has an ingredient in it that is action. It is not what we think love is. It is not even what we say love is. It is what we do. It is action, not what we say. It means that we give children the support and care they need until they are able to be out on their own, and then we let them go. There would be no ownership of the children. They would not be *my* children. The children might even be brought up by a group or community, thus giving them the experience of many different people and situations, not just one or two people as it is now.

Transformation—A New Beginning

I say the most perfect surrounding in which to raise children, at least in today's world, is by individuals who have had experienced a transformation. When we were born, we were forced into a secondary unit of living which is knowledge or thought. We are forced to live in a thought, knowledge invented world. The only manner in which we can step out of that world, I say, is through transformation. Because this conditioned world is so solidly ingrained in us, the ending of it is the only thing that will allow the manifestation of transformation.

Transformation can be described in many different ways. Some who talked about transformation also used the word *mutation.* I use the word *transformation* because mutation has a violent connotation to it. When we say *mutation*, it sounds like we are putting it in a blender and mutating it into a lizard or a zombie or something else.

When I hear the word *transformation*, it means *end;* then *new.* There is only a blink between *end* and *new*, and there has to be that blink. There has to be that little division point where it's "I am dead," and then "I am alive." That is the reason why we all need to die psychologically before we can live. The person we are now is the one that we invented, the ego. We are no longer the natural action of intelligence.

We were speaking earlier of raising a child, and that child is you. You have lost your natural action of intelligence; and if you have a child, the challenge is to raise the child and yourself at the same time. That is the real challenge. Most parents already think they know how to be themselves and know how to raise a child, yet the reality is that most parents are stuck as children themselves and don't know it. They are psychologically two or three-year-olds trying to raise a child. Once conditioning gets a hold of a person

42

around the age of four, that person is stuck there forever until or unless there is a transformation. We are all children having children.

We are conditioned to believe that we are meant to grow up, get married and have children. That is part of our programming, and once we have children, we are conditioned and programmed to bring them up to be successful. Yet, we are living in an insane world; therefore, a successful person would then be on the top of the insane ladder. Once people reach success, they want to keep things as they are so they can keep their successes thereby promoting the insanity to continue. Success is just a measure of our insanity, and those who are considered unsuccessful are just as doomed. They are stuck as well. The latter ones might have a greater possibility of transformation, though, as they are on the *outs* of society. Yet, either side is the same, successful or unsuccessful, because they are all still stuck in the conditioning of what society deems to be right or wrong.

Being 100 Percent Responsible

The *need to be right* is the cause of suffering. Any form of disagreement in a conversation with anyone is you having to be right. Seeing that presents a huge opportunity for you to shake hands with yourself, so to speak, when you see this need to be right in yourself. But what do most people do when they have this discontent or anger in a conversation? They blame the other person and hold onto their *being right* position.

When you start to see your need to be right and catch it in the action of it happening, that is the beginning of growing up, of bringing up your own child—you. When you begin to accept *what is*, that is maturity. You won't say "I don't want it to be like that," and you won't say "don't be that way."

It might nice to have it your way and be the boss, but if you can't, just move on and see what's next. If you continue to want things your way and have to be right, you will be stuck. You will be stuck as a little child. You will have tantrums, fight, kick, scream and want only to get your way. If you can see yourself in that as it happens, you will see that little child you are stuck in. That is not being mature; that is not an adult. That is a little child who has to have his way. You can tell because that child will never give up. If you have not grown up, how could you possibly be able to raise a child? You are still a child yourself, and that is the way of our world—children having children.

The most difficult thing to see and say to yourself is that you are the world's worst parent, that you failed at raising yourself and that you failed at being a parent. First you need to discover that it is you. Just look at yourself without any comparison with others. If you do this, you will discover that no one else could have screwed up your children as badly as you did. No one else could have screwed up as badly as you did because they are *your* children. You are the one who had them, brought them up and conditioned them to be the same as you.

This is not about opinion or judgment about what a dysfunctional parent is. It is not about comparison or that you did it better or worse than another. Speaking the truth about yourself to yourself is taking 100 percent responsibility for everything that has happened in your life. It is not the other person who did it. It is not even the child's other parent that is to blame. It is not a matter of blame at all. Responsibility does not include blame in it. It is seeing that you were responsible, period. If you blame another, or yourself, for even one little sliver of it, you will be missing that one little sliver; and that one little sliver keeps you fragmented; therefore, you will not be complete. If you blame another, you are giving them part of yourself, for they are now included in your failure which makes you less than 100 percent responsible.

That is why you probably will be the same sort of person again and again because that is your failure. If you could see that where you are blaming someone else, that is the place where you are missing yourself and are not whole. This is very tricky, and yet it is so huge. My guess is that no one sees this because if they did, they would never blame another person again for anything. This is very difficult to see especially when we are caught in the *blame game*.

Creating a Partnership with a Child

As I have stated before, the child is ninety-nine percent more intelligent than we are, but we don't realize that. We think we are the smart ones and know more, so we immediately start to train the child to fit into this world, which actually takes away the child's intelligence. We teach this intelligent being to be a trained and conditioned robot like ourselves because we think that is what we are supposed to do. We do not see what we are doing.

When we speak of a transformational way of being in partnership with a child and to do as the child does since the child has the intelligence, I do not mean to go to the child's level. A partnership takes away levels and keeps each person equal. You would need to speak to the child in the manner they can relate to, and that is saying to the child "we are equal."

You might get down on your knees and speak with the child, not in a baby way, but in a way a baby can hear. You are also inviting the child to stand up and walk with you. You are not altering your way of being with what you are doing and saying. You are not speaking gibberish to the child. You are using words in the language you normally speak and in a manner you normally speak although the words might be adjusted to fit the child's understanding. You are then relating to the child in a partnership way, and you are not altering your way of being to be the child's way of being. If you alter your way of being to accommodate the child, you are lost and done for because then the child owns you. Children are intelligent and they can figure out quickly what they can do to get their way with you, and they will do it. Then you are lost.

The crux of child rearing is being able to have a partner instead of a baby or a child. This is difficult to do because our world almost demands that we own the baby because the whole world is lost in ownership. We own *our* husband or *our* wife. A partnership does away with ownership. Everyone is equal. In a partnership you speak the truth with the child. You don't fill children with lies and then tell them not to lie. How insane is that? If you speak truthfully with them, they will learn truth. The children today are taught lies. They are taught that they must talk nicely to people and be polite, and sometimes that includes lying, which is what we are telling them to do. They can't say somebody is fat because that is not nice. We tell little lies so often that we don't even hear our lies.

A young girl comes here to stay sometimes, and when she gets up in the morning, I tell her how pretty she is. Then she spends an hour putting on make-up to cover her natural beauty. Because we are stuck in the lies we are told about the need to do this or that in order to fit in and be that thing called female or what a female is expected to do, we cover up our natural selves. And the parents encourage that because those are also all the things the mother did when she was that age. That makes it OK that she does it and OK the children do it, too, thus keeping the entire insanity going.

We didn't know what to do to raise ourselves, and then we think we know what to do to raise a child. We continue the insanity of the past by teaching the child the same things we were taught without looking at those things, without seeing what those beliefs are doing to us, our children and the world we live in.

When I speak of raising a sane child, I am saying for the parenting to not come from already knowing what a parent is supposed to do because all the things we know and have learned come from thousands of years of conditioning. If we act from *not* already knowing, then we will not act from all that has come before. If you can, find another person you can interact with who doesn't already know everything so that you discover what it means to act from the unknown. That would be a perfect experiment. In doing this with your children, you would be dealing with them in *the now*, for *now* is always new. But as you are now, you are meeting them in the moment with the old.

Creating a Partnership with Yourself

The key to creating any partnership is to begin with yourself. You need to create a partnership with yourself and start from there. Even if you don't know what a partnership is, start creating one by speaking out loud, "I create a partnership with myself." That may seem odd to you, or maybe you don't think you can do it, and you may resist saying it. Don't add an "I guess" to it or "maybe" to it. Don't even say that you intend to or that you will create a partnership as the words *intend* and *will* put it in the future.

When do you intend to do it? State in *the now* "I create a partnership with myself," and then watch what comes up as you are saying that. Even if you don't think you can do it or don't know what it means, say it anyway as saying it sets up the automatic intent for it to happen.

If you look and see that you don't know how to do that, say "I can't do that." Speaking the truth of it will open up a blank space, a slight pause and a waiting to see what will happen. State that you don't know, and that is all. If you add an "I guess" or a "maybe," then there is no clean slate. The past is still there wanting to come in.

You don't know what creating a partnership means because it has not happened before. It is new. The only way to see that is to state out loud "I don't what creating a partnership means" and then watch to see what happens. That is a first action of being in partnership with yourself. Then you can ask "am I a partner with myself?" and look to see if you are or not. Most likely the answer will be a "no." Then you might see a small opening of being a partner with yourself as you become aware and see yourself in that very moment. If you have any resistance or discordance or anger or thoughts about it, there is no partnership there.

In saying "I create a partnership with myself," you can then look to see where you are not a partner with yourself. You will see what a partnership isn't. You start then being complete by creating the partnership, and then look to see what is missing. You cannot put the pieces together from the pieces because there are too many pieces, and each piece will cause another piece to be made. Each layer will demand another layer, but if you start being complete with all the pieces; you can see the parts that are missing. The *complete* I am speaking of is the partnership of a fusion of self. At first you will not know what a partnership is, having never experienced it. A partnership with yourself is like having a true friend who tells you the truth. In fact, it is that.

A true partnership has no division psychologically. There is no fighting with yourself because partnership is a movement of togetherness. If there is any resistance, then you are fighting with yourself. A partnership is a fusion with yourself, and that brings all the fragmented parts and pieces together. We have all been fragmented into thousands or maybe millions of pieces with all the traumas and dramas of life. So, the first step needed to fuse with yourself is to create being a partner with yourself. Then you will realize that there will not be any difference between your movement and your thought about the movement.

A fusion is the merging of the multiple sides of you that are arguing and fighting internally. We are all multifaceted, having many scattered pieces. Only a fragment can be fragmented. Nowadays it is even considered a must to be multitasked, to be able to do many things at once. This scatters us even more psychologically. We are at war with ourselves, and with some people this war is going on constantly internally. Fusion of self brings all facets together and makes them into one cohesive being. It joins of all the pieces, and it happens with the movement of creating a partnership with yourself; and the partnership, the fusion of self, is the ending of this cycle of insanity. It fuses your physical being with your psychological being. You will move in unison, one movement.

In the Bible it is stated "those whom God has joined together, let no man put asunder." That is what a partnership means, and you are the God that the book is speaking of. So, if you put yourself together with you, no one will be able to pull you apart. Sometimes I like to use words that are unfamiliar, like *asunder*. That causes a slight pause so the person can then ask "what does that mean?" Anytime we can stop the robotic thinking, we are in *the now* — in the moment we need to question it. Asking questions is also a slight admittance that we don't know everything, and then there is a possibility for that movement towards *I don't know anything*.

The fusion of your parts, the partnership with yourself, is the ending of this cycle of insanity. When you create this partnership, you fuse your physical being with your psychological being, and there is a movement together with yourself. You will move in unison, one movement. Now this will look and maybe feel stupid in the beginning because you will no longer be controlled by your conditioning. You will be in the moment with intelligence, and that is far different direction than the world is now moving.

Now, this will look and maybe feel stupid in the beginning because you will no longer be controlled by your conditioning. You will be in the moment with intelligence, and you might notice you are doing some things that appear to be stupid, but you are actually creating yourself new. It is like you will be creating a new wheel instead of using a wheel that has already been invented, and the world is going to ask "why create something that already exists?"

The world will remind you how it is supposed to be; yet, you will see that old wheel doesn't work for you anymore. It doesn't fit into your world anymore. So you will be creating a new wheel, a new life, and at first it will be awkward. This might be extremely difficult as you might not want others to think of you as dumb in trying to create a wheel when there is already a wheel.

Discover Yourself in Relationship

You discover yourself through relationship. When you get into a relationship and you argue with somebody, it is really yourself you are arguing with. You are a person who argues. But you people don't discover that. You think the other person is the one who is arguing, and you blame them.

In creating your partnership and looking to see any place where you have resistance or discourse, you will find that is where you are not in partnership with yourself. That resistance will tell you that is the place where you are fragmented.

Listening can only happen when resistance is gone, and resistance disappears when belief is gone. Belief causes a closed mind. When belief is gone, there is an open mind. Seeing your resistances will open you up to fusion, a partnership with yourself. If there is discordance, it is with yourself. You are the one who caused it to be, and if you blame another person or blame the experience, you are not seeing you are the one causing it. Then you are fragmenting yourself even more. This causes more discordance and resistance instead of bringing the parts together.

You need to be serious about all of this, and yet most people are not. When you see you are not serious, you need to become serious 100 percent. Once you get to 100 percent seriousness, you get to the other side where ecstasy, creation and intelligence live.

Being serious sometimes implies sternness and hardness or always frowning. *Serious* can be a fanatical kind of thing, but I am speaking of seriousness as in doing something 100 percent, putting your whole self and being into it. If you actually discover you are not serious, you will become serious, and once you move through the seriousness you will discover what life is, what living is.

If you are always trying to become a partner, you will never become a partner. *Trying* is a non-action word. You are not doing, and trying will only cause more trying. If you are trying to become a partner, then everything you do to move into the partnership will cause another thing that is needed to be done. Like peeling an onion, always more layers will be there. It is like having a million pieces of a puzzle trying to fit them together to make the whole.

If you create the partnership to begin with, you have the whole thing, and then you can see what is missing. Trying to become a partner and creating a partnership is essentially the same thing, yet with *trying* you are starting with the pieces whereas with creating you are starting with the whole. The whole will manifest from completion, and from the pieces, pieces will manifest. This is a tiny distinction, yet the tiny is the whole world because it affects your whole life.

"Humpy Dumpty sat on the wall. Humpty Dumpty had a great fall. All the Kings horses and all the kings' men couldn't put Humpty Dumpty together again."

They were working from the pieces and could not make him whole.

Death of the Ego

If you were to die psychologically, which means to let go of all your beliefs, from that death you would observe all the things that make you dead and keep you dead and all the things that make you alive. The context of this is *death*. That is why truth works so perfectly—it ends the lie. If you stop there, at the end of the lie, there is a space which you could call *death* because there is no continuation of the thought. That is the place of the death of the ego.

Continuation of a thought happens when we have a belief. Beliefs are not true, yet we think they are. We were told something or we read something, but we had no experience of it. Once we hold onto a belief, we will keep defending it and reinforcing it. That just goes on and on. It might disappear for a while, but it comes back around again and again. If a death occurs by ending a belief, there is a space, and from that space we can create something new. But if the belief doesn't die, from where there would have been a space, we bring forth another belief or we reinforce the belief we had.

That is the insanity of our world. We have beliefs that it is OK to kill another person if we declare they are against us. We even give honor and praise to those who kill other people in the name of this or that cause. People justify and condone killing. We live in a violent world, and all of that comes from holding onto beliefs.

Life Lives in Questions

When you come to a place where you don't know what to do, ask a question. Asking questions releases beliefs from taking a hold on you. The bible states "ask and ye shall receive." It is not saying to ask for money or riches or things. It is saying that the process of asking a question will open you up to receiving. When you are stuck in your beliefs and probably in pain and suffering, question what you are thinking and believing and ask "where did that come from? What caused me to do that?" Ask what caused that particular thought to come around now. Do not look for an answer; wait and let an answer appear. Notice what was happening when the thought came up. It usually has to do with something, maybe tiny, that sparked your memory. Just let what comes forth happen, and do not force it.

If you look for answers, you will get stuck in old beliefs and cycle thinking. Often the best answer is "I don't know" since that leaves a space which will allow the answer to come. To keep all of this alive in you, each answer would contain a question within it. If you stop at an answer, you will be stuck in belief. The questions keep you alive, and the answers keep you dead when you hold onto them. Life lives in questions, and death is in answers.

Living is a continuing process of asking and looking and asking and looking. Real life is in the answering of the question, but it is not an answer if the answer doesn't have another question inside of it. I am not talking about just repeating endless questions or *who*, *what*, *where*, *how* and getting stuck in judgment and blame. That is not what I am speaking of. Yet, if you find yourself starting to go into a loop or find yourself going into the past further and further, then a way to break free of that is to speed up the process.

See it all happening very fast. This actually causes it to slow down.

It is important to find that space between the question and the answer where intelligence can come through. If you are in a loop or repeating questions without that pause, you are stuck in belief. The question brings forth the space if you pause or stop after asking a question, or you might ask another question such as "where is that space?" That is an exit door exiting out of belief into an empty space. It is like a hall of mirrors. You keep bumping up against yourself in many different forms, and you are looking for the way out, the exit. The exit is the questions and the space after. We were trained and taught in a linear manner which has no end. If you are going on in a linear manner and you find a space, the space breaks it. Asking a question, pausing and creating a space will break that line.

Ending Ties that Bind

Now, ask a question to find that chain between you and your parents, and break it. Although *break* is not the correct word as it has violence in it, it is an ending or dissolution of the chain. Do the same with your children to find all the cords and beliefs that hold you attached. Cut them. That leaves a space for intelligence, love and truth to come through. Cutting the chains might seem scary as this is a form of dying psychologically to our parents and our children. We will be a different or new person without the beliefs we have been holding onto our whole life. Breaking the chains of belief our parents handed to us from their parents and that we handed to our children will break the conditioning of our insane world. Once you break the chains, you are standing on your own. You are free.

There is a time when children need to leave the nest and stand on their own. It used to be called *cutting the apron springs*. Often there are times when that might naturally occur, but it is missed or hindered. The child may have graduated from high school and have a job or might talk about moving in with a friend. Instead of the parents supporting this, they might argue or say "no." These are definite times when a child is ready to leave the nest; but we either miss this opportunity or we don't want it to happen. Then the natural breaks don't happen. Suddenly we realize we have a 30 year-old still living at home. Then a forced break might need to happen, and by then it is more difficult. When the break point happens (either a natural moving away or a forced move), and the child falters or falls, then the parents think they need to help them or hold them up. If that happens, you are lost even more because that is teaching the child that when they fall, someone else will come and help them and that they don't need to figure out what to do to fix it themselves.

In a partnership, all of this has to do with intelligence interacting. It doesn't have anything to do with a parent being a parent or a child having a parent. There is a small distinction needed when listening to *what* I am saying needs to be transformed into listening *with* what I am saying so that listening is all encompassing.

When I have conversations with people, I watch their actions because that is where listening will show if something is heard. Speaking and listening are an action of intelligence, and there is a movement together. Most people are doing one thing and thinking a different thing, therefore, there is no walking together with the two. If speaking was from intelligence and it was heard, there would be a moving together.

If you see you are negative about something, look to see if maybe you are negative about many things, and then maybe you will see that you are negative about everything. Most people cannot see the 100 percent. They think they are a little bit this and a little bit that and cannot see that it is *all* of them in *all* aspects of their lives. Seeing your negativity Is not a bad thing, it's just noticing that is what you are. No judgment or opinion is included if it is to be 100 percent. Be what you are 100 percent, and that is the completion of it—the ending of it. This is not to point to someone else and say they are negative; although, in a partnership it might be something you care to discuss together. However, if there is blame included in it, such as saying that the other person is the negative one, you no longer are looking at yourself. Negative people's first reaction will be to attack the messenger even though they might call it defending themselves.

Some people think that to have a good relationship they need to fight. Some people even want to fight so they can kiss and make up. They say that *makeup sex* has more intensity in it, and that might be because in a fight people often say the things they have been holding back from saying, which is a violent way of speaking the truth. When the truth is spoken, it releases energy, and then energy is gained. Possibly that is why the fight started. When people start to speak the truth and the other doesn't want to hear it, they argue it back and forth, sometimes never ending.

If you'll notice, you often have the same fight with a person throughout the whole relationship. It is the same thing repeatedly. During the fight, both people speak things they thought they couldn't say any other time, and they think they are being heard. Neither person can hear the other when there is a fight going on, and that is why fighting never ends. The perfect time to speak your most bothering thoughts is when you are not angry. However, you might think that will start another fight, so you hold it in. When we hold things in, we blow-up when something is said that pushes our buttons. Then fighting is an all-consuming relationship.

Bailing Out Children

Children need to learn the natural consequences of their actions. You can still guide them without stopping them. Parents think they are protecting their children when they bail them out of the consequences of their actions, but it isn't helping them, and it could be a hindrance. Let them learn on their own, and if they fall into the hole, just watch and see how they get themselves out. If you help them out, you have taught them that you will bail them out, and then they are not learning for themselves. In fact they might do things just to get you to bail them out, to get your attention or to test the limits. If they have been trained that way for many years, and now you want to stop it, expect that they will get upset if you don't bail them out. They have not learned how to get out themselves and believe they cannot, so bailing out our children is a detriment to them. Doing what you believe a *good* mother should do is possibly the most damaging thing for the child, for you are acting out of belief, not *the now*.

We don't want our children to have difficulties, yet we do the things that keep them having difficulties. We might think we are doing the best things for the best reasons, but the reasons keep the problems there. The child might be fat or slow or have an addiction or be lazy or messy, etc., and we make excuses for them and do things that keep them exactly as they are. We perpetuate the things we would like for them to not do.

Sometimes it is actually because we like to save them that we want them to ask for our help, and they may learn to feel helpless unless we take care of it for them. Parents will sometimes act in a manner like that not even realizing what they are doing. It makes us feel good to be needed, and who would need us more than our children; so this is a difficult thing for us to stop doing. It is a form of enabling. It is keeping children down so we can come along and save them. The strings or cords I spoke of earlier need to be broken *now* because as time goes by, they get more and more difficult to break. They go from strings to cords to wire to chains; and not only that, these attachments grow and get tentacles, and the tentacles grab and strangle us.

When we are always helping our children, we are keeping them as children; and even though it seems like they would like us to keep doing it, on some level they realize it is keeping them as children, and they resent us for it. Then, after a time, they resent us if we don't help them, and they resent us if we do. This is how many parent/child dynamics continue far into adulthood and possibly continue until one of them dies.

In a partnership everything stays balanced. If we see there is something that might destroy the partnership, then we tell the other partners about it. We do not support it, and we don't make excuses for the behaviors. The main ingredient in a partnership is trust, and trust means 100 percent trust. If there is no trust and we are in a partnership, then what is the partnership based on? You might ask how it is going to work if we never do trust.

We Are Still Children

The problem with current adult relationships and the relationship we have with our children is that we have never grown up. We are still children behaving like children. We are *all* adult children. We get angry over little things because of issues we never cleared up as a child. We are still that child acting like a child. When another person says something that makes us angry, we revert to the age when that issue first came up and never was resolved.

When we get angry, listening stops and there is no actual discovery for ourselves. We don't realize when a person says something which makes us angry that the person is correct in saying something about us we might need to hear. Yet instead of hearing it, we get angry, and then we become the little child and act from there. If we could see this when it is happening and listen with that other person and not revert to childhood issues, at that moment we might find a great gift. However, because we get angry, over time the other person learns not to say certain things or do certain things they know will trigger anger. We then lose that opportunity all together.

In you can, get permission or an agreement in a partnership with the other person to speak anything that is going on with you. This doesn't mean the other person will not get angry, yet it might assist in anger not happening, or it might be a place to start with this process. Even if there is that explosion, there might be that small opening of permission to speak the truth which may allow it to be heard.

Keeping secrets and hiding things only cause the relationship and partnership to fall apart. If you have to manipulate, control and force things, all is doomed. You find that you cannot sleep at night, that you worry about things, that you are always stressed, suffering and in misery. That is what happens when you keep things bottled up inside.

You need to keep yourself clear which means to speak things out, and speaking them out in the moment of the happening is preferable. But if you are with someone who stifles you, or you are stifling yourself because you feel you cannot talk with the other person, it traps both of you. Even if you cannot speak things as they are happening, at least take some time later, maybe once anger is gone, and then speak it out. Some people may keep journals to write what they cannot speak, but that is not as clearing as verbalizing it. Because we are trapped in and by words, we need to speak them.

If there is any discordance or anger within you about what is being said, then what is being said is true, and you don't want to see it. If it were not true, you wouldn't have any reaction to what is said. It wouldn't bother you at all. This is difficult to see because we want to say it was somebody else's fault, that the other person caused the problem or what they were saying is not true. So if you notice anger or discordance of any kind, stop and listen to what is being spoken. Then ask yourself "what is causing this anger?"

Then ask yourself out loud "where is this anger coming from?" and "why am I getting angry?"

It is always something that is within you. It is not another person who is causing it. So, look and see where it is, why it is and what is causing it. I am not professing going into a deep analysis because analysis only makes things more complex and often just gets into the cycle of thinking that goes nowhere. Ask the question and wait to see what comes.

Anger is a defense, a way of blocking the other person from seeing things you don't want them to see. It puts up a wall so that you can feel more protected from that childhood pain. You may feel that if you allow the other person to say what they need to say and you listen, there is a chance you will let them into your life too closely. That is frightening to a lot of people.

If you do things so that your spouse or child will not get angry, or you know they will get angry if you do certain things, that causes harm to both people as well. That is another form of keeping secrets and lying. You know if you say something, they will get angry, so you don't say it. That is now bottled up in you, and if it cannot get out, it will cause stress and eventually harm to both of you.

End Doing Things for Them

Sometimes it seems easier to do things for the people in your life rather than keep asking them to do it. Also, it is easier to be quiet when you really have something to say. However, taking that easy way is really the hard way in the long run.

In the situation with children when asking them to do something like clean up their mess, you often end up doing it yourself, and then they learn to expect it. No matter how much you ask, they know that you will do it eventually, so they just let it go until you do. Usually there is no appreciation that you did it. It is now an expectation, and then it starts to grow. They do the same thing in other areas of their lives. The more you give in, the more they demand.

In order to break the habit of doing things for everyone else, you need to start *not* doing things for them. If you have been doing for them for a long time, it will be more difficult to do because they now expect it. They might even get angry at you for not doing it, yet you need to not do it. You need to move in the other direction with it. This is where I say you need to be the *worst* mother in the world, because it is important for you and for them to stop catering to them. Doing the things they need to learn to do doesn't teach them anything other than that they can get someone else to do their work. They are not taking responsibility for themselves, and you are enabling them, allowing them to be that way. If you can see how this will harm both of you, you might then see that being the *best* mother by some standards is often a detriment to the child and to yourself.

What you create is there for you to see even if it is negative creation. You created it to be there. If you are in a situation you created, such as the messy child or spouse, look at what you created and create something new. *Create* implies not having been before, so if you have tried something already and it hasn't worked, don't keep doing that same thing. An act of creation is not figuring something out, although the act of creation and figuring it out do walk hand-in-hand at times. Try different things to see what happens. An act of creation comes from asking a question and then being still and waiting for an answer. Don't assume an answer or go read a book to find out or ask a friend. That is figuring it out. Ask yourself what can assist you in this situation and then wait. Take a pause, complete the question and then stop. If what comes up is new and not from you thinking it out, that is an act of creation.

A partnership agreement which allows each person to say what they need to say without anger or criticism will bring up topics they have not felt free to bring up before. It isn't just that the parent speaks and the child listens. It goes both ways. The parent also listens to the child. If the house is messy and there is partnership, it means that I clean my mess and you clean your mess; and what we do collectively, we clean up collectively. That really does break the *mother does all* or the wife *does all* syndrome. Many husband/wife relationships are the wife taking on another child in the form of a husband, and it is expected that she be his mother.

A Child's Imagination

Even though it seems innocent, teaching children that Santa Claus, Easter bunnies and tooth fairies are real is actually teaching them a lie. We are saying to children that these imaginary beings are real and that they can expect to get things from them. That is not innocent, and it is a disservice to children to foster this.

It is important to foster children's imagination, and it is important for them to be aware that what is happening in their minds is not real. Show them that imagining things is fun and exciting, and it is just in their minds. Imagination is that there is a Santa Clause, but that doesn't mean there is an actual guy with a beard who will be coming down the chimney and bringing them gifts on Christmas day. If you don't let the imagination manifest into children thinking it is real, you are telling them the truth. Imagination is in the head/mind, so that is where children need to realize it is coming from. Otherwise they might grow up with magical thinking, thinking that there are imaginative beings that will bring presents and make their life better, and they will never live in the real world. It could be understandable that we want to live in the magical world since our world is so insane.

If children can see the distinction between the real and the imaginary and then be shown how this world is insane, they can then come through that into a sane reality that is better than living in an illusion. If we could invent children's games bringing imagination to games rather than competition, games would be more enjoyable as well as showing them how the world works and how this is a world of opposites and upside down—something like Alice in Wonderland.

So children can have play or imagining time and realize it is only in their heads. If the imagination and games fostering imagination were championed in this world, that would bring forth a world of creation rather than invention, invention being a continuation of the past. Imagination is the entry point of creation. If you shut down that entry point by making imaginary beings into a belief, children grow up being scared to death of the devil and hoping for a God to save them. That is imagination being put into the physical world.

Developing Games for Children

Discovery games that could assist the child would probably assist the adults as well and possibly even more if the parents are open to allowing the child to create the game as they go. Most children are already in this realm of possibility, whereas the adults are probably more closed because grown-ups are conditioned already to the world being as it is and not seeing a possibility for something new.

It is difficult to speak of creating a game to assist with transformation and bringing about sanity since that is something created in the moment. That kind of game would be difficult to pre-determine. The child will be the one creating it as you each go along. So, the game would need to be one that can be created in the moment, as it is happening and not be pre-determined.

Sometimes creating games might assist children with learning about how to live sanely in this world although I would use the term *experimenting* or *discovering* rather than games. When someone thinks about a game, it is usually about winning and losing, and then we are back stuck in dualism/opposites. Games are usually about competition, and competition is the beginning of violence.

Creating some games where there were no winners or losers might work for teaching children not to be violent. Very young children's minds live in the world of imagination where they are already in creation. They don't have much of a concept of win/lose or right/wrong. So any game that could capture that part of them is one they would revel in. It is important, though, for them to be aware that they are using imagination, and it is not real.

By inventing a game called *Win/Lose* you could show children the experience of winning and losing. That would be experience in this world of dualities. They can be shown competitiveness, the thrill of the win and the agony of defeat. They could experience the winning and losing one right after the other, and allowing them to be aware of both would be the point of the game. Something like that might allow the child to see other issues which are causing pain and suffering, such as the need to be right, which is a huge problem in our world.

Even if we take care to bring up children without competition, they are going to eventually get out in the world where competition is a very big part of the world, so they will experience it. So this game/discovery will assist them as well in knowing what to expect in this world of insanity.

The goal of this game would be to show children that when one wins, another loses. If they can fully feel the experience of losing, they might then appreciate how others feel when that happens. Then compassion might develop. When they are fully aware that one goes with the other, they would discover we cannot have win without having lose in the world of duality and separation we have now.

If they can experience *win/lose* almost simultaneously, they could have the awareness that they go together, and compassion would be a natural action. That might eliminate competitiveness. The game would be to show the child or adult that we all experience the same things. We have all experienced the pain of losing; thus it might assist the child to create compassion for another person. These kinds of things will show all of us that we are living in a world of win/lose or success/failure and the pain we experience because of these dualities. Perhaps, we can then come to a point of balance where the experience of winning is the same as the experience of losing.

People are starting to be aware of the effects of competition on children and the world. To succeed in today's world we have to stand on someone else; and if standing on someone else is OK, soon we have to wipe our feet on them, too. Then we start to kick them. In other words, it keeps getting worse.

With winning and losing, we were taught to keep score and know who is ahead and behind. We were taught competition is a good thing to teach our children so that they will be able to succeed in the world. This is true since the world is set up that way now. It is also the way to teach them sorrow, pain and sadness because that is what comes with competition.

Success or Failure—A New Look

Currently we struggle in our lives to learn, and then we take pride in what we have learned. We use that learning to struggle and make money, and then we take pride in our jobs and accomplishments that bring us the money. Others want to follow the moneyed people because they want to have that money as well. Thousands of books have been written about how to get rich "if you just follow what I did." That does work for some—following the rich person's formula. Almost all people who are rich had to struggle hard to get there, probably failing many times along the way, and most people don't want to struggle that much. A lot of the rich people had a time when they lost everything, and they had to start all over. That is something most people don't want to do either. So, even with a formula it is a struggle.

Just look at the life of Abraham Lincoln or Thomas Edison, for example. They failed many times, yet they never let the failures stop them from continuing. If you can accept your failures, call them failures, not be ashamed of them or hide or excuse them, you will not repeat the failure because you have seen the failure completely. You are not accepting failures when you make excuses for them, and because of that you will continually repeat the same failures. Accepting failure completes it, and completeness ends it all.

Many of you are doing what you consider successful, and the only part that is keeping you from actually being successful is that tiny little failure. If you find that failure and see it completely, then the success is there. But you cannot find the failure until you call it *a failure* and see it completely. Of course, that is assuming you don't let the failure stop you from continuing or cause you to give up.

Seeing the failure doesn't mean to stop doing what you are doing,

In some cases the failure is what causes something to be a success, and even then that needs to be seen as a failure for it to be complete. Showing children the right answers or even for them to have right answers, unless that answer includes a question, needs to be avoided. That goes for the adults as well. Remember that all of life lives in questions, not answers. The questions are there to be answered, but the answer then needs to have another question. Death, stagnation and insanity occur when we get the answer and stop there. You then keep repeating that as a formula for doing something, and you get stuck in that rut.

When you do something and it brings you something more, such as money, success, romance; etc., you will keep doing the same thing again. That usually doesn't work a second time, and yet we keep repeating it hoping that it will work again. It is almost like an addiction. The first time or maybe the first few times we get a great high from something, and occasionally that high shows up again. For the most part, though, we get pain or suffering from it after the new wears off. Yet, we remember that high and keep seeking it repeatedly. Our thinking tells us we found something, and we keep repeating it, hoping that it will continue to bring the same effect. It doesn't.

The cliché "insanity is doing the same thing again and expecting a different result" is how we are living now. We keep repeating the past, which is a failure, expecting it to be something new or different. We live our lives based on what we were taught, and what we were taught doesn't work. We are failing, and we won't admit it.

Let's take the example of guns. There probably was a time when guns were needed for everyday survival, and perhaps we could say that guns were successful in getting us to where we are now. But they are no longer needed for everyday survival, so to keep on having them or thinking we need them, puts us back in the past and keeps from being able to move forward. So we need to say, "OK, guns served their purpose. Now let's put them away and start something new." As long as we hold onto them we are stuck in the past, and cannot move out of violence. They were once a success, and now they are a failure. Seeing that will end the need for guns.

Taking Care of Adult Children

What can parents do who allow their adult children to live with and take care of them even if they don't want to? That happens when we take ownership of our children, and they are *our* children. That begins to cause children to not take responsibility for themselves. There is an expectation on the part of the children that *their* parents will always take care of them. When adult children have come to a point in their lives where they have failed, parents will then allow those adult children to come back to live with them. Sometimes the adult child never leaves. This situation has become more prevalent in recent times. To continue saying *children* when you are referring them after they are grown only deepens their problems. They are no longer children.

Years ago most children knew when they left home that was it and there was no coming back. Now it is common to hear about adult offspring living with their parents and sometimes even multiple generations living together. One cause of this might have to do with parents not learning how to say "no" to their children when they were little. They have spoiled them. Also, some of it might be due to the female shifting from the stay-at-home mom to the working mom and her guilt of not being there for the children, so she makes up for it by spoiling them and not saying "no" when she needed to. Parents give wishy-washy answers which the child learns very quickly means *if I bother her enough, she will give in.*

There is a distinction here between a "no" when they want something versus a "no" when you are stopping them from doing something harmful. I am speaking of the "no" when the child wants something, and we end up getting them everything they ask for. That is detrimental to both the child and the parent. The child expects that the parent will give them whatever they ask for, which is usually true; and then when children get older, they still expect that.

Sometimes the parent does say "no," but then they add an explanation or excuse to it which the child soon learns to get around. They get a "no," but they know it is not true. They can figure a way to get it to be a "yes." Soon the child will continue to ask, beg and plead because they know you will give in to them. If you could learn to give a definite "no," they would know they cannot come back and continue to ask and beg. You need to say "no" without any excuse or explanation. Just say "no," and certainly don't say "maybe later." It might seem heartless to do this, but that is *tough love,* and that is for their ultimate good, and yours. Children can learn that there are limits and to take responsibility for themselves. If you keep giving them what they want, they don't learn to get it themselves.

Often the parent actually wants a child to fail, or not be able to make it without their help, because the parent needs the child to need them. They believe the child cannot do something without their help, and they will cause that to happen and to continue to happen. We are the ones crippling them. They say they are going to go out and run a marathon and we say "OK honey" and then shoot them in the foot. Then they keep coming back and we keep crippling them. By that, I mean that we keep giving them money or help or letting them live with us. That is crippling them to the degree that they are not able to function on their own. Yet, we as a parent feel that if we say "no," then we don't love our children.

The truth is that we do not love ourselves, so we cannot love our children. If we did love, we would prepare the world for our children and ourselves rather than preparing ourselves and our children for the world. Everything we do is done to fit in. We are preparing them to go out and function in an insane world rather than creating a sane world for them and us to live in. We have an insane world, and the first thing we do is make our children insane in order for them to fit in the insane world and that just continues, reinforces and deepens the insanity of the world. In order to end the insanity, we must break the link of insanities by creating a world that is worthy of us and our children. We allow the world to be as it is, and then we see if we can fit ourselves and our children into it.

Most people might agree that the world is insane, yet they exclude themselves from it. They say it is someone else, not them, who is insane. People cannot see their own insanity, and they think it is everyone else's insanity but not theirs. Yet, it is everyone on the planet who is insane, not just a few, not just those others out there. It is everyone. And every generation is getting worse and worse. As the population increases so does the insanity of the world.

Transformation of ourselves will end the insanity, and it needs to be a collective movement in order to move us out of the state we are in. Every drop of sanity that goes into insanity causes the insanity to shrink and sanity to grow. In a broad sense, sanity is the ending of war and all violence. Violence is the result of thought, belief, religion, marriage, guns, ownership, competition, etc. Sanity occurs when thought is no longer in charge.

Weed Your Mind

Let's say that every person on the planet has discovered that war start with a frown. Then if people noticed they were frowning and asked themselves what they were upset about, that would clear it right up. I liken asking that question to completely turning and plowing up the ground for a garden. The next day you come out and there is a little weed, you would see it immediately and pluck it out. It is like that. You would notice the discord in you immediately and pluck it out of your thoughts. This might be a *pie in the sky* way of living your life, and that is what I am looking at—a mind that is so clear the smallest weed is plucked out before it can grow. That weed is a belief. That weed is violence. Most people have a forest full of weeds which makes it difficult to clear the mind because there are so many weeds.

Insanity is any discordance, any resistance, any anger, any fighting. Sanity is the ending of all of that. I get little energy bubbles that run through me when I look at the possibility of people actually being alive and aware because if they were alive and aware the minute the frown happens, they would see it.

Right in the middle of you is a perfect orchid. It is there, and the only problem is that you have to plow up the weeds that are surrounding it.

We are the world. The observer is that which is being observed. You cannot see something in another unless it is also in you. However, you cannot see it you because it is hidden, and when you get yourself clearer, it will be very clearly seen. Even the smallest discordance will be seen. We have many escapes to get away from our disturbances, and the more you don't run away from them, but acknowledge them, the more sensitivity you will cultivate.

To consider doing all that while raising a sane child is difficult until you can first see your own insanity. You start to become sane when you see that you are the insanity of the world. This may seem too massive and impossible or that it is too overwhelming. The positive side is noticing how impossible this might be because you can see it is all encompassing. Seeing all of that is huge because almost no one discovers that or even gets to that point of seeing it. Instead people have excuses for everything. The ones with the worst excuses are the ones who brag about their children being doctors or lawyers or big executives or other successful people. Those people are the greatest contributors to the insanity.

The greater the success in a failed entity, the greater the failure is to that person. The further up the ladder of success one goes, the greater is the insanity. When we see the enormity of it, we realize we cannot do anything about the children or about the world until it comes down to the individual, to each person. It starts with you. When you switch from your negative self to your positive self, your negative self will say that it is impossible. It will say that your whole life is this way, that the whole world is this way, and it is absolutely impossible to do. Then the positive side will say "OK, so what do I do first?"

The key here is asking a question and ask using the word *what,* which causes a more open answer than the word *how*. *How* questions are for people who want to be given a road map. *How* people don't want to investigate it themselves. They want to be told what to do and how to do it. And, the question isn't "what can I do about them," or "what can I do about this or that." The question to ask is "what can *I* do about *me*" because I realize I cannot do anything about something or someone else.

We are the perpetrators of wars, each one of us. We will know we are a failure as long as there are still wars, and we will know we are still causing wars if we frown. That is looking at ourselves in the smallest detail of our violence—a frown. We will see violence, all the way from war down to the frown. This is something each of you needs to discover for yourself.

All that I have spoken with you are words. What I care for you to see are your actions. That is what the words are pointing to—action. Intelligence is in the action. It is not in the thought or the words. Intelligence is not in the description, and it is not in the understanding. It is in the action, the action which is behind the words. There is a difference between a judgment and a distinction, and that can be seen or heard in the tone of your voice.

Learning the Lies

Until around the age of four, children see everything, the whole thing. Their minds have not yet been filled with the programming. There is nothing we can hide from them. We tell them not to lie, and then they see everything we do. We tell them not to call someone *fat* when the person is actually fat. We teach them to lie when we teach them to be polite. They see all of our actions, which speak louder than words, and they see the actions which contradict the words; and then huge confusion takes place. They see us lie, cheat, manipulate and how we use excuses to justify things. They see us blaming others and not taking responsibility, and yet we tell them not to do those things. They see the truth in the actions, not in the words. The children learn from our actions, and we are teaching the children to live in a world lies and illusion.

Most people or parents do not realize they are lying because they have excuses for the things they do or say, which justifies to them what they are doing. They don't see their actions as lies, or they know they are lying and say it is just a little one or it is for someone's good. People are so accustomed to lying that soon they don't realize their whole life is full of lies. They are not even aware of lying because lying is such a big part of the way they live their lives. Children learn how to manipulate us based on the way we have taught them to manipulate, and they will use those same manipulations against us.

Let's say you have a problem child who is always in trouble, and in the past you have always bailed him or her out, always made excuses for them and never let them have their consequences. That is why some children are a problem. They haven't been allowed to have their own consequences or take responsibility for themselves.

To break that chain, children need to start taking their own consequences and responsibility. The parent taught the child to live in this illusory world by saying not to lie or steal or cheat, all the while the parents are lying, stealing, cheating, manipulating and justifying. The illusion is not that you are lying, stealing and cheating. The illusion is saying you are *not* lying, stealing and cheating while you are doing it. You put yourself out there as the person who doesn't do those things while doing those things, and that is what the child sees. All lies are an illusion, an illusion invented by virtue of telling a lie or not saying the truth. When you do one thing and say you don't do that thing, you are living in an illusion.

Want Is a Four-Letter Word

Why would a parent teach their children to want something? It is usually because it is easier. If we give them what they want, they won't yell and scream or continue to nag. We teach our children to want things, and then we get upset for what it is they want or don't want. So it is probably one of the greatest easements for the parent not to teach the child want to begin with. Want is the weak sister of what is needed and necessary. Is it necessary to have Wheaties instead of Cheerios? There was a time in our history when "what do you want to eat?" was not even asked. Children ate whatever was prepared for them, and there was no discussion about what they wanted. Then things shifted, and now we do all the things that are spoiling the children, teaching them to want things. In many cases it has to do with what we didn't get, so it has to do with what we want as well.

Somewhere along the way things shifted from children having no say in what was going on, to almost the other extreme where they have total say about everything. It used to be that children are seen and not heard to now where the child is the one in control of the family, and the parents work their lives around them. When the pendulum swings far in one direction, it will inevitably swing back too far in the other direction. A lot of parents were brought up being stifled as children. It is almost inevitable that if parents were stifled, as in the old seen and not heard days, they probably said when they grew up and had children that they certainly would not stifle them. So, it has gone to the other extreme. It has gone from being silent to yelling, and it has not come back to the center point yet.

Creating a partnership with the child would be that middle point where both the parent and the child have equal say in things that happen in their lives. Possibly, the parents expected they could make it balanced, but it hasn't come to that. In a balanced way of living, the child would learn the times it is appropriate to speak and times when it is appropriate to be silent. This would happen as part of the natural actions and consequences of their lives, not forced or contrived.

In the past, children were almost sub-human and now they are considered superhuman. The obvious perfect place of balance would be 100 percent respect for the child and the child's respect for the parent in all circumstances. I am not talking about teaching a child to be polite since that just teaches them to lie. I am speaking of a respect without forming rules around it. Teaching them to be polite has to do with teaching them the right things, depending on how the parent saw it, such as the rule that children were to be seen and not heard and rules from religious upbringing.

This gets us back to the transformation of the parent because a transformed set of parents would be balanced and would have a clear view of the child. The parent would see that a child would gain when needed and lose (have consequences) when needed. It is difficult to say how that would manifest as the parents and child would be walking together in the now, for in the now things manifest from intelligence and not from figuring out what to do. However, we are currently starting with not only an unclear mind of the parent; we are also possibly starting with already conditioned young or older children.

In many cases, people have an older child, and the place they would need to start is obviously with themselves in the domain of language. Begin to see the words and the manner in which you speak. You ask, "What do you want for breakfast?"

The child says, "Cheerios."

Then you get upset and yell, "We don't have Cheerios."

The deterrent to all that consternation is to not ask the child what they want and to not teach the child to want things to begin with. But once they are already taught, you would need to take the word want away from them or request that they remove the word want from their life.

When we are dealing with people who are already trained and conditioned, their minds are so full of their history that any suggestion they remove anything from their lives is extremely difficult. Most people want to add things to their lives, so all they can do is repeat their history. Part of that conditioning includes wanting to want as we believe that wanting something is our motivation to succeed. We are taught to want to be better, to want to achieve more in our lives and we believe we need to want things. Want is attached to more which is attached to money, which is attached to success, which is attached to our competition and which we ultimately believe will bring us happiness.

You might be asking yourself why you would give up wanting things. Want is also attached to pain and suffering. If you were to remove the word want from your language, you would remove a lot of negative things in your life. You don't see that want brings along with it the opposite. The don't want comes with it, which is an illusion, a polarity of opposites. Teaching children to want is part of all the problems we have with children today. They have gotten to where they want everything. Want is a road which we really don't need to go down.

Giving in to children usually starts with the parents being too busy or having too many obligations, and the child gets left out of the equation. So the parents feel guilty and compensate by giving them whatever they want. Also, it is a way of keeping the children quiet and out of their hair while parents are dealing with the things going on in their lives.

The Buddhists follow a doctrine that includes a statement regarding desire or want, saying it causes all suffering. Want can only do one thing, want, and its attachment, more, can only want more. Those two words can only do what those two words say. They are usually found together as in want more.

We are taught to want things and that will make us happy as if things could make us happy. We don't realize that with happy comes sad. Happy is only a fleeting thing when sad isn't there. We are taught and accept that we are supposed to want happiness for our children, which is part of forcing them into sadness. We do not realize the consequences of that insanity.

Happy is one-half of sad, and when we are heading towards happy, we are heading towards sad as well. Want is always directing us towards duality. We want a good thing, and we don't want a bad thing, not seeing that the good and the bad come together as all opposites do. And when we get what we want, we want more of it. Getting caught in the happy/sad cycle is also included in depression. Depression is a result of bouncing back and forth between happy and sad.

Wanting and seeking happiness often cause addictions. When we first did the thing we became addicted to, it was a happy experience. Yet most likely that was only fleeting, and then it became, or still is, a sad situation which don't want to have anymore. Yet we are still hoping to get that happy feeling back again, so we keep doing it. This is also where more comes in because we want to do more of what we became addicted to in order to find that happy we had at first. We are stuck in the cycle of wanting happy and not wanting sad.

What people are actually seeking is peace; not as in the duality of war and peace, but peace of mind. Peace lives outside of suffering. So if you care for peace, you would remove want from your life as want causes suffering. If you don't want something or anything, then there is nothing to be bothered about and that brings peace. When we want something different than what is or when we don't want something that is there, we become bothered. That is why I said to remove the word want from your life and from your child's life. You can start by saying "I take the word *want* out of my vocabulary and out of my life."

Notice how many times that word want comes up in your thinking and your language. It might disguise itself in such a way that you don't realize it is a want because the mind can be tricky. You might say that would like to have a certain thing, and that is the same as want. You might think something is nice or good, and that thought could possibly bring up you wanting that thing.

Take out of your vocabulary all of the wants that you have placed on the children. You want them to succeed, you want them to be happy, you want them to grow up and find the perfect mate, you want them to have children, and you want them to be healthy. Give up all those wants as they carry with them and all the don't-wants as well. When we are living in the illusion of duality, we cannot get one without the other. Removing want might seem like an impossible thing, and possibly it is. Maybe you can do an experiment of looking at all the wants you have and see what shows up.

If you did take the word want out of your vocabulary, there would be a natural progression towards caring. You might realize that you care for something to happen without the more forceful want of it. The word care is gentler. It doesn't force; it comes from a quietness of your mind. You offer a space of care, and if what you care for doesn't happen, there is no sorrow or anger about it. If you do this experiment, you might find that you fail often because removing want from your vocabulary will be a difficult thing at first. When that happens, just look at it and see that you have failed thus far. Seeing your failure is all that is needed to succeed.

"Yes" or "No"

One of the most important things for a parent to learn is to say "no" when it is appropriate. The key to saying "no" is a "no" that doesn't have any anger in it and has no feelings with it. A "no" is not meant to stop children from discovering when they are investigating their world. A "no" is appropriate when a child is asking for something he or she wants. Saying "yes" to those requests reinforces that you will always be there to give them things and will continue to give them their wants. Saying "no" is one thing that could save both you and your child much suffering. Saying an appropriate "no" allows children to take care of things themselves and to stand up on their own; and if they fail, which they will many times, it teaches them how to deal with failure and the lesson of consequences. Most adult children have not learned this. They want things, and they keep on wanting someone to give it to them, usually their parents. The fact that we keep calling them *our children* when in actuality they are not chronologically children reinforces their childish wants.

Children often think the world is against them when they don't get what they want, and then they feel like a victim. That is because they don't know how to deal with life on their own and take responsibility for themselves. This malady started with the parents always saying "yes," and worse were the ones who said "no" a few times and then eventually gave in and let them have what they want. This is even more devastating because children then learn all the forms of manipulation it will take to get you to come up with the "yes" they seek; and they will use those manipulations the rest of their lives as long as you allow it.

Say "no" firmly without any anger to it. Say it as just a statement of finality. Do not add any excuse. Any excuses you add will be tools they will learn to use to finally get what they want. For example, if they ask you if you can take them to town, do not say "no, I have work to do" because they can come up with something to continue to ask for once that excuse is complete. Then you have to come up with another excuse. The truth is we don't want to take them to town, or we want them to learn to do things on their own.

Like the anti-drug commercial used in the 1980s, "just say no." Have that tone of finality in your voice. You will definitely get a "why not" from them, at least the first few times if they are used to you giving them excuses. Just say "because I said no" without any further explanation or reasons or excuses. It might take a while, but they eventually will learn to be able to get the things they want on their own or not have them.

I am not saying to never say "yes" to them. Actually I encourage "yes" to be your way of life. However, when children ask for something they want, that is the time and maybe the only time to say "no." This "no" stops the action of children and teaches them to take responsibility for their own lives. There is a huge distinction between the "no" I am talking about here and the "no" when we stop children from discovering something. This latter "no" is a violent action. It is said to limit and control. I know this can be confusing, yet the distinction lies in your intent. Instead of the "no" in the case of them discovering something, we might join with them in the discovery. We could protect them from what we were stopping them from doing or talk with them about it. This way they can learn on their own about life and its consequences. In the former "no," it is to a question they are asking in the form of usually wanting something. Saying "no" in that instance is for the child's own good.

This might be similar to something which has been termed *tough love*. It might be difficult to be tough because we were not taught that ourselves. That is what *tough love* is— tough on both the parent as well as the child. It is a change for both of you, and change is difficult. Where there is a manipulation between two people, such as when one is getting something from the other, it is like a string energetically connecting the two people. That string holds them both in that same manipulation. Children know if they pull this string, they will get what they want. That is the manipulation.

Usually both people want something, and they are both pulling on different strings seeing which string will get them what they want. The parent wants the child to do something, and the child wants something else. The key is to realize that it is always a two-way thing. When one of the strings we use to manipulate the other to get what we want is broken, it is broken both ways, and that manipulation doesn't work anymore. Then they have to try other strings. You will need to be very aware of yourself and what is going on so that you can stand firm because children/adult offspring have learned throughout the years exactly which string to pull to get what they want. That is not a *bad* thing. It just is how they were taught and probably by you, so it will take compassion and care as you are breaking the strings.

We were not taught how to say an appropriate "no." We do not know how to say a firm "no" without there being some guilt or feeling of not being a good mother or father. Most of us were taught that a *good* mother and a *good* father give their children what they want. So, what I am saying goes against what we were taught, and that is exactly what I am talking about when it comes to raising a sane child. We were all taught by insane people who were taught by insane people. If seeing that what you were taught might have been a detriment to you, why would you continue to pass that on to the children?

I am looking for finding a way for us all to move together as one movement, one partnership. In the way things are now, everyone in a family is moving in their own direction, and there is usually no movement together. The father is doing his thing, the mother is doing hers and the children are all doing theirs. Usually this is the cause of stress and discord within the family rather than bringing them all together. Since there are so many personalities going in different directions, usually one parent takes control and is the director of them all. In the past this has been the male or father, and now things are shifting to the female or mother. Either way, it is the same.

Being Attuned to Your Child

A lot of people are not taught how very important touch is for the child. Of course, touch needs to be appropriate, just as is the word "no" for their wanting something. A gentle, caring hug is what a child needs. Touch is similar to the topic of tone. Children can hear how we say something. They can feel that as well. If we touch them harshly or inappropriately, they can feel it. So, it is important for the touch to be without any anger or violence in it.

There is a theory that we can spoil children if we pick them up when they cry, so this often keeps a parent from holding or hugging their child at all. Again this requires a parent to be aware of the child, to know when the child is using a cry to get something, a manipulation, or if they actually need something. As you can see, this is a very fine distinction. We need to be aware of the reality of what is happening. There is a time and place when picking up and moving around with the child is imperative and a time when putting them back down is equally imperative. The only way to know this is with the awareness of the parent for the child's needs. It is difficult to see this unless we are aware of the child when he or she is trying to get attention or learning ways to get us to do things and when they really need a hug or carrying around.

It is difficult to say exactly when holding a child would be appropriate and when it is spoiling the child. That determination is delicate. The problem arises because is too difficult to say when to do it and when not to because a rule has been made, and parents went to the far extreme with it. Parents are not aware of themselves, let alone the child. Since the parents didn't know when it was appropriate to hold their, they erred on the side of not holding the child at all. This has been going on for a few generations now, and we have a society that is touch deprived, and then children act out in inappropriate ways in order to get attention and touch. It is often a smack on the butt or something else violent. The thing about a rule is not to follow it religiously. It is important to check and make it a rule of thumb to check rather than just set it in stone. We check with the child. This is part of being attuned to them. We then get an awareness of what is going on with the child and will be able to tell if they are in need of something. It always gets back to being aware and attuned first to yourself and then to them.

If we have not been touched when needed and in the manner which is needed, how would we even know how to administer that same thing to the next generation? We are an individually raised group of people. Everyone is separated. Even within the family, things are separated. *He* is a boy and he needs cars. *She* is a girl and needs dolls. That separation is there, and it doesn't get broken by touch for touch's sake. Not only in the home is there a lack of touch, for even now in schools, they don't allow the children to hug or hold each other. We are in a vicious circle because if all of a sudden we begin to start touching, we get in trouble; and if we don't, World-War III is on its way.

Sometimes children are crying just to be crying. They are learning about their own voices, and crying is part of that. It takes a parent who is attuned to the child as well as being attuned to themselves to make these discernments. If you are attuned to yourself, you will know when you like to be touched as well, and again this is something most people are not shown in their own childhood. It takes being attuned to yourself before you can be attuned to your child. Being clear with yourself, speaking the truth of yourself, your own sensitivity and value of yourself keeps you balanced and in tune. When we are attuned to ourselves, we can then be aware and attuned to someone else.

We have all been successful in learning the manipulation of our parents. We know what we need to do or say to get the things we want. We have also been in need of attention and have been ignored. We have experienced both sides of it. The same is true for our parents with their parents. We are all dead/unaware, and we were raised by parents who were also unaware. Now we are seeing if life is possible after that death. We are seeing if we can create life with something other than sex; seeing if we can create it with ourselves. Can we impregnate ourselves and become our own parents by speaking the truth of ourselves? If we can't, we stay children psychologically and rely on others. We are all adult children, never learning to stand on our own. We are children who were raised by children attempting to raise children.

Living Your Labels

When we are with our children, we step into the role of mother or father, and the whole context of the relationship is in the role we play. If we have a negative relationship, stressful or strained, that makes the actions and reactions negative, stressful or strained. This goes in both directions as we will respond in a negative way and so will they.

Sometimes there are a lot of feelings associated with the interaction—often sadness, sorrow, anger, suffering and pain. Some people notice when they are away from the children they act differently than when they are with them. When the children are around, the parents shift into the children's reality and are no longer themselves. The parents leave the person they are behind and become the mom or dad.

This is especially noticeable with mothers. They are usually brought up with the idea they will grow up and have children and become a mother. They are taught all the things a *good* mother would do and be, so they develop in their minds the kind of mother they are going to be, the kind of children they are going to have and how the relationship between them is going to be.

All of that is put together in a context called *mother*, and it is not based on reality. It is based on fairytales and imagination. When the real shows up, when the child is born and grows up and is *bad/good* or whatever it is, then the whole idea of *mom* gets blown away, and we are stuck with the reality of it. When the reality begins to conflict with the concept of the whole thing, that is where sadness, sorrow, anger and all the suffering happens because it is not matching our idea of what it should be or what we had planned. We want the children to be the image that we have set in our mind, and when they are different, there is resistance to it; and we want it to be the way we envisioned it.

If the child is in a very negative lifestyle such as drugs, depression, etc., we are sad that our child is going through such a rough time, and we want to help him or her. In doing that we get sucked into where they are. Often the child does want us to come where they are to rescue them; and, also, at the same time they may push us away.

Even if the child is not in a negative place, a disconnection is still there between the fantasy family of your imagination and reality. There is often a big division between the concept and the actual, and then we have a conflict between the two. When the child grows up and goes away from home, often our minds go back to the imagination again; and when we get back with them, the reality of it usually hits us again. They are right there, and we cannot wave our magic wand and make them the president of the United States or a CEO of a major corporation or a doctor or a lawyer or whatever else we envisioned them to be. Sometimes we want to stay away from them because it is too difficult to see the reality of who they are because of the disconnection between the imagined and the real. You need to realize that this is unfair to children as they are who they are, and it does not have anything to do with the image you created for them.

I suggest you switch your attention from you to them and watch what it is that they do so that you can see what your reactions are. Most of the sadness and pain is caused by your being stuck in re-action rather than action. In other words, you are just repeating your history. True joy, true ecstasy, and a true life come by living *your* life. When you are repeating your life, rather than living it, it is dull, mundane and boring.

Children usually are not aware that they continue wanting you to rescue them. It is just expected based on past history and the way things have always been. Speak with your children and let them know you expect them to start taking responsibility for their lives and to be able to deal with things as they come up on their own. This goes back to the partnership that needs to be created between you and the other, that each of you needs to take responsibility for your own life. If you keep helping your children, they will not learn how to do it themselves. It seems difficult for a parent to do this, to allow a child to experience the consequences that life gives them and let them fail. Parents don't want to see their children fail, to be hurt or be in pain. They think that *helping* is for the child's benefit. It isn't.

The role of mother or father was determined by you when you were a young child, and that role was added to throughout your life. Little girls' toys are geared towards them eventually growing up and having children. Little boys' toys are usually geared towards them growing up and going to work or playing sports or another adult male activity. You grew up accepting those roles, and you live your life based on that. It is possible to start clearing that conditioning, and it begins with seeing that is what happened. Then it is important to make the statement that you no longer accept the role of mother/father. You are not denying that you gave birth to them or conceived them, but you do not have to have them as *your* son or daughter, as *your* child, as *your* responsibility or as something that you *own*. Think what happens in your mind when you say *my* son or *my* daughter. When you put the word *my* in front of anything, it causes an ownership.

You can give up your ownership by saying "I give up my son" or "I give up my daughter." What you are really saying is you give up the "my" part of the son or daughter. The ownership of them is what you are giving up. You are giving up the illusionary part that owns them which in turn allows them to stand on their own and be able to grow up. Then, in each moment see if and how you are still holding on to ownership of that child.

In order to discover every place you are holding as owning them, you must first see that you are owning them and then give that up. Then every instance of where you own them will start showing up, and you can then say "oh, yes, there it is," and you can just give up those instances. It can happen in a flash. It is not something that would take the rest of your life. It might happen in one fell swoop. Once you see it and make that statement, it happens. You are breaking the chain. There will be residue, like the little bit of growth that comes out of a tree trunk when you cut it down. Those little growths that may show up will need to be cut off. When you hear yourself say or think "I am their mother so I have to do this," that needs to be trimmed.

There might be some confusion at first from the children as they are expecting you to act or be as you have always been. They will be facing some large movement that they need to make; some adjustments they might not be willing to make as now they will need to be responsible for their own lives. When they fail, and they will, they will not be able to come to mommy or daddy to bail them out. It might be appropriate for you to speak with the children about this and let them know that you no longer are going to bail them out, and that they are now responsible for their own lives.

When they know you will always bail them out, it is almost a guarantee that they will fail as this is part of the dynamic being played out. They fail and you bail them out. They know this, often without full awareness of it, or they may be fully aware of the exchange. They might think they can go ahead and do what they want because they think their parents will bail them out if something happens, and that something usually happens. Neither one of you is doing it *wrong* or at fault. You are all living out of a programmed expectation brought about by years of conditioning and over generations. It is a reciprocal thing in which all of you are caught. The manipulation is always on both parts in order for it to be manipulation. You are both manipulating each other to get what you want; even if you don't know you are doing it. Otherwise, it is just begging if it is not on both parts.

Cutting the chain might be difficult for the parents as well, for they often have a need to be needed. It is often more noticeable for mothers as they tend to be the more frequent caregiver. Mothers think if they continue to care for the child that will keep the child tied to them, and that is exactly what does happen. This creates a problem for children as they will always need the parents, and they will never be able to grow up. In the long run, the child will end up resenting the parent for doing this because as long as the child comes to the parent for help, the parent gets to be the helper, the big shot, and the important one who knows more than the child does.

This need to be needed also promotes the feeling of being a *good* mom or dad and a sense that you are doing a good thing or that you are a good person. Some people have a belief they can heal their children or even the whole world. The need to be needed starts in the place of loneliness with people realizing that they are alone; that they do not have anyone in their lives, and there is a hole inside them they don't know how to fill. They feel that the more they help other people the more people will like them and be drawn to them, and they believe that will fill the void. Having a whole bunch of people in your life does not mean that you will feel complete or not alone. It is just a need to be fulfilled. When you do something to get something, that is not working out of integrity; and ultimately you will end up getting nothing. When people are in that place of really needing another, there is nobody there. In the place of complete despair, complete alone and giving up, there is nobody there to pick you up. So that need to be needed is a false sense of having somebody there. You feel like the more people you help, the more people you will have around you, which is true. It often becomes a burden, though, which you resent, and you resent them for coming around asking for your help. On some level you know that if you stop helping others, you will probably lose them as friends or make your children upset, so you continue to help them and resent it.

The manipulation continues because both sides don't want to end it. You are getting your needs met in being needed, and they are getting theirs met by getting something. It is all a manipulation on both parts, and it is not beneficial for either one of you. It damages all of you in the long run. On the other side, it may apply to you also. Maybe you are getting something or getting help from your parents.

The breaking of the chain can go in either direction and will always go both ways, either from child to parent or parent to child. You might be able to see the patterns you have that you got from your parents, the patterns you label as *good* or *bad*. You can see the manipulations you used to get something from your parents, e.g., money, love or attention, and even as an adult, you may still be doing it. Then you might be able to see the same manipulations your children are using with you. These actions came from your parents, and you passed them on to your children, and you are the key to ending it. You are the chain, and if that chain in you breaks, then it is broken in both directions. When you release yourself from being your parents' child, they are also released from being your parents, and when you release yourself from being your children's parent, everybody is released from being owned. That's the real benefit of doing this. You have the opportunity to see the origin of it from your parents and then the result of it in your children. Remember there is no blame here. Your parents got it from their parents who got it from theirs, and you passed it on. Seeing that and taking responsibility for it is not *blame*.

We accepted our parents' concepts about *mother*, *father* and about the world, and then we passed those concepts on to our children. So now we can watch our parents and see that we are doing the same things they did, and then we can watch our children and see how they are doing it, too. Once we see we are all doing the same things, we can watch that without getting upset or sad or angry. Just observe that this is what is going on without trying to change it.

The awareness or observation of it will bring about the transformation of it. If you do have a reaction to seeing all this, just observe that as well. No blame is needed as we are all in the same situation, the same manipulations. Watch how you are pulled to either appease your mother or father or stand up for your child or whatever happens. Notice the trained and conditioned aspects of being a parent or a child as you are being both. Chances are you will find out they are the same.

Sometimes it is easier to see how the children are like our parents, and we cannot see that we are the ones who are the conductor, just as in electricity. You conducted your parents into your children. You are at the effect of your parents, and your children are at the effect of you.

World Peace

One of the big questions parents have for their children is what do you want to be when you grow up? But then, we often direct them in the way we want them to go. This is the same with setting goals, which are also *wants*. We are conditioned to want goals and to set goals in order to succeed. That is also something the parents want the child to want, making it a double *want*. They want the child to be successful, so they foster these wants on the child. They want them to have a good job so they can have a big house and a nice family and be happy. Yet, often parents leave the child out of this, so they are forcing a set of beliefs and wants on the child until the child believes that is what he wants as well. So, if you want your child to be a doctor or a football player or whatever you want and then push the child in those directions, your *wanting* is causing violence against that child.

Yet, many people think that is what they are supposed to do to be a good parent. This is another example of us trying to force children to fit into this insane world rather than allowing them to be who they are. It is the world forcing us through the beliefs we got from our parents that they got from their parents and back for thousands of years. We want the boy child to be tough and grow up to be a *man* and do what a man does. It is the same for the female child that we want to grow up and be *a woman* and do what a woman does. We teach them to care more about money than peace in the world, peace for themselves and peace for other people.

If there has to be a goal, which I say is not necessary, let it possibly be to create world peace. Creating world peace would always come back to the self. World peace would include seeing the failure of the world as it is. It would be the ending of everything we already have and starting the creation of something that has never been here before. World peace has never been here before. World peace would include everyone being equal and balanced and no one having more than another. There would be no one above or below; we would all be the same. We don't know what that would look like since it has never been. The beginning of that is to speak out loud, "I create world peace." We could say that is a goal, but it is not. It is a function of caring about the world and ourselves. It would benefit everyone, so it is a care, not a *want*. When we include *care, want* disappears.

It seems that those who are promoting world peace are the ones who don't have any money or any power to make any changes; yet each one of us has the same opportunity and ability to create peace. It is an act of linguistics, not an act of power or money. Actually, money and power will end when world peace begins. So each of us could have world peace by saying, "I create world peace" and speaking it anew each time you say it. See the possibility of it as you speak it, and don't just repeat it.

World peace would probably not be accomplished by working on issues like "Save the Whales and Dolphins" or "Feed the Children" as often these are just distractions people use from looking at themselves. They think they are doing good deeds; again not seeing they are stuck in duality as *good* comes with *bad*.

World Peace can only happen with the seeing the truth of ourselves and speaking it. Now, if we are working on *saving the whales* while we are working on seeing the truth of ourselves, then that is a perfect action. We can be working on anything; it doesn't matter what it is. If we are looking and seeing the truth of ourselves, we are moving towards world peace.

We are all living in a violent world, and none of us sees it is each of us who is violent. We always blame everyone one else. No one is at peace with themselves, and we blame others for that. Peace on earth begins with each one of us, and that begins with seeing that you are violent and that you are not at peace. For all of us to stand up and take responsibility for ourselves, see our failures, not make excuses and not blame others, would bring world peace.

Labeled by Schools and Doctors

Children today are labeled with all sorts of disorders, and the schools and doctors push the parents to get the children on drugs. The most common label is ADHD (Attention Deficit Hyper Disorder). The children are too active to sit still for classes, and instead of looking at the problems of the current teaching methods and school curriculum, the authorities say it is the child's fault. They then want to give children drugs to keep them from being energetic children. Children are naturally active, and in today's society they don't get enough release of that energy. They sit and watch TV or play video games; they don't go outside much or get any other kind of physical activity.

A young boy once came here and stayed in the mornings until it was time to drop him off for school, and before school, I would take him outside and have him run and move around. We made games out of throwing rocks in the backyard. This allowed him to release all the energy that was built up, or at least take the edge off it, so he would then be able to sit still for classes. Children aren't given much exercise any more. They take busses to school, they sit all day in school and then they go home and do homework and watch TV or play video games. This is done by many children daily, and eventually the child no longer has any desire to exercise or even go outside and play.

These children who are diagnosed with ADHD or other disorders are probably the children who have escaped the trap of the conditioning or at least are attempting to. By the trap, I mean they didn't *die to themselves* psychologically as most children do. These children escape our effort to condition them into the robots that we have become, and they have a delayed or secondary *psychological death* after the first one around age four. The second one comes around

13 to 18 years of age. Their ADD/ADHD is them resisting being part of the programmed masses. Those who escape the conditioning even after 18 years usually become outcasts or rebels. They haven't conformed to what is expected of them, so they live outside of society. It is not that they are bad or evil; they just refuse to give in to the rules. Eventually, though, they give in because it is so difficult to live in the world being on the fringe of society.

The children who are labeled as ADD/ADHD are ones who are resisting being molded into what we want them to be. Most schools are doing things as they have been doing them for years because they have not adjusted or become updated. Most schools now have computers, but they still teach in a slow and dull manner that is boring. It was boring when we were children, and we were not brought up with all the fast paced activities that the children of today have. It is crazy to force a child to sit still for a long time and learn useless rules and facts and figures; and then when they are not able to or willing to, we drug them to make them learn. Instead of fixing the problem of the schools, we think we need to fix the children.

It all goes back to bringing up a sane child. We ourselves drive our children insane by continuing the teachings of our parents and their parents and an archaic school system. With the children we were not successful in conditioning, the school takes care of that. If they can't quite take care of it, then the doctors and schools have labels for them—ADD or ADHD. Then the children are given drugs to take care of it, and in many cases the children become addicted to the drugs, or they seek other drugs to keep them insane. They are forced to fit in, and the society they are forced to fit into is insane.

The thing called Autism is slightly different than the labels of ADD and ADHD, as that does seem to be a reaction to vaccines and other environmental factors. There could be a combination of ADD/ADHD and Autism, or there is a confusion between which is which. One of the characteristics of an autistic child is that they don't seem to have feelings or that they do not sense other's feelings. This seems to be an extremely advanced child because they have avoided feelings. They are actually what I would call a transformed being, or at least close to it because a transformed being has no feelings, such as anger, sadness, happy, etc.

Feelings are not the same as emotions. Emotions are real. Emotions are *love*, *compassion* and *care*. Feelings are not real. Feelings are in the world of duality—the world of *happy* and *sad*, *good* and *bad*, *right* and *wrong*. A child without any feelings has a greater possibility of looking at things and seeing the reality of them since feelings are attachments we add to things that are not real. We judge something as good or bad, right or wrong and those are the feelings we attach to the experience.

A distinction needs to be made here between a transformed being without any feelings and a person who is labeled a psychopath or sociopath as those terms bring up the image of someone without any feelings. A psychopath or sociopath does have feelings, the feelings of anger or revenge or the very high sense of being right, and they are going to make the world pay for what they feel. What they might be lacking is a feeling called remorse, yet they do have feelings. A transformed being has emotions, but they do not have feelings.

See the Lies

The key to transformation of ourselves is to see our lives and our memories without having any feelings or attachments to them; to see them as they actually are. The attachments are judgments, opinions and feelings that have anger, sadness, shame, pride, etc. We assume we are right, and we attach that to what we say; and when someone suggests we are not right, the anger comes up because we think we are right. When someone tells us we are not right, we defend ourselves usually by attacking the other person verbally or otherwise.

If we are shown to be wrong, it may seem to us that everything we built in our lives was wrong, and it is almost like we would then be dead. It is a death of the ego, and that death is exactly what is needed as everything in our lives is a lie. Yet, we still want to hold on to our attachments, thinking they are the right things to do or the right idea. If we could just let go of all the feelings, transformation has a possibility.

When I see people letting go of their attachments in the workshops I do, there is a rippling effect of energy to it. It is like someone letting their clothes just fall off their body in a rippling motion, and they are standing there perfectly naked psychologically, not physically. When you live a lie, it is like the clothes you wear to hide your body. Your true self is hidden behind all the lies you tell.

Lie and *truth* are actually not opposites; they are both actions, action words. They are not in the duality of *right/wrong, good/bad*. A lie is the protective energy field we wear around us like our clothes around our bodies. It has been called our ego as well, for they are the same. When you begin telling lies at an early age, you can literally picture yourself putting on clothes, like a body bag that zips all the way up over your head, and you then live your entire life inside that bag. Seeing that your life is a lie would be like unzipping yourself out of the bag.

Seeing that your life is a lie is seeing the truth. When you tell a truth, some energy is gained. It doesn't matter if it is a small or a big lie you told the truth about. If you robbed a bank or you slammed the door, saying you did it is telling the truth. Sometimes it is best to start speaking the truth about the smallest things in your life. Saying your whole life has been a lie is speaking a truth. Saying that you are a violent person is speaking the truth. Saying that you don't know anything is speaking the truth. Saying that you are insane is speaking the truth. These are all truths, but they are the most difficult ones to speak. So start with the small truths, such as you ate the last cookie or you slammed the door or you broke the dish. That is a start.

Sometimes I ask people to repeat a truth they haven't seen yet. For example, I will ask them to say "I am a robot," or "I failed," or "I don't know anything" because even though they don't see the truth of it, saying those things opens up the possibility for it to happen. You never know when it will hit you, and you never know what will cause it to hit you. Maybe some of you who have gotten this far into linguistics can see this in yourselves, and maybe you could see it from an early age; and there is a part of you that didn't give in to the conditioning or has been fighting against it all of your life.

Dropping the lies in your life can only happen when you see the futility of your life. Not when you say "most of it." Not when you say "I can do this or that." It's when without a shred of sadness or sorrow or regret you can see you have been and still are a robot—a completely failed, lying, cheating, stealing robot.

112

The greater the stage on which you show your fool, the greater is the death of your stupidity. The more of yourself you put out, the more of yourself you get back. Yet, no one wants to look like the fool. We all want to be seen as smart, and we all want to be right. We will defend our need to be right all the way to killing people because of it. And those things we are killing others for are just lies that were carried down from generation to generation, and we continue to believe them. We are fighting for things we believe, and belief lives in memory, in our thoughts. Beliefs have judgments and feelings attached to them. They are lies.

The Need to Be Right

Having to be right is the core of our consciousness; the ego has to be right; yet no one can see that or can admit it. If they do notice it, they have a feeling or attachment to it or a place they still hold onto being right in one or more places. That is their stopping point, the place they are still holding on. Our whole life is a reinforcement of *being right*. We get A's in school for having the right answer. We are rewarded throughout our lives for being right.

By the time we are four or five years old, we are already programmed. We are already beaten into a psychological submission. We have already given up, and we join in and believe the program/conditioning of our parents and society. From that point on, we continue to reinforce those lies, those beliefs. Our parents might have been the ones who taught us the beliefs, just as they were taught by their parents, but we are the ones who continue to reinforce them and defend them as if they are the right way to live. Then we teach those things to our children, and they continue to reinforce and defend them.

Your parents trained and conditioned you, and you accepted it. You continued conditioning yourself by making yourself right and by doing everything they said for you to think and do. You accepted and followed the rules and did what you were supposed to do. This is placing the responsibility where it belongs—on you. It is not up to your parents to help you, nor is it your responsibility to help your children. We are all responsible for ourselves.

We resist going through normal, through crazy and through insanity to get to sanity, and the only way to get through to the fountain of sanity is through normal, crazy and insane. This takes a huge level of courage because it is combating the very core of your being. The very core of your being is violence, and the first step of violence is *having to be right.* We resist letting go of being right because it is our core, and we feel like we would die if we did let go of it. It is really a letting go of everything because our whole life is made up of what we believe to be right. The need to be right is to protect our knowledge, everything we know. And what we think we know is all based on beliefs, which are lies.

End the Insanity

All that I speak of here is done by the function of intelligence speaking into knowledge with the expectation that knowledge won't grab ahold of it and run. Perhaps knowledge will take it as an experiment instead of believing it. Knowledge is the way we have been taught, which is from learning from what other people had to say and believing it.

People acting from intelligence would experiment with things and discover everything for themselves. Knowledge destroyed intelligence. Intelligence cannot be understood because understanding is of the mind, which is knowledge. Intelligence is in what we don't know. If it is known, it is of knowledge, not intelligence. Intelligence is having a clear mind, and a clear mind has no attachment to memory. That doesn't mean intelligence doesn't have a memory. That just means it doesn't have an attachment to memory. Intelligence uses memory when necessary and drops it when it is not.

The pathless path of transformation is in the path called *truth* because truth is the destroyer of the path, and the path is a lie. The truth destroys the lie; and a lie destroys the truth, as well. It is a balance, like a balance of life and death. You can't have one without the other.

Everything on our planet, everything that we are, is the mirror image of reality. Right/wrong; good/bad and all dualities are the mirror image of reality. Knowledge is the mirror image of intelligence. Invention is the mirror image of creation. This is why our present life is an illusion. It is made up of what is not real. Many times people see the truth, but then they can get lost in it and begin repeating it without seeing it anew each time. When something is repeated, it is no longer true. People sometimes have enlightenment or even a transformational experience; then they stopped there and started to believe it and repeat it which then develops its own illusion. Someone sees the truth, and they start to tell everyone about it and keep repeating it until it is no longer real. It is no longer the truth. That is how religions started, and that is how they continue to this day. They might have been started by someone who saw the truth, and that was the truth for them. The repeating of it is not the truth. It is a lie, a belief.

In every truth there is a lie and a lie in every truth. The lie is the ending of the truth, and the truth is the ending of the lie. If you tell the truth about something that you had previously lied about, telling the truth of it ends the lie. If you repeat a truth, it then becomes a lie because it is only a repetition. Only something said in the moment of it happening is the truth, which then ends the truth.

If you can say "I am insane" without any attachment of feelings such as judgment or opinion and see it as 100 percent truth, that will end the insanity. If there is any attachment to what you say, it is not a truth spoken, and the insanity does not end because that is a lie telling a lie. If it is an actual truth you are speaking; you will suddenly see it, and that is the ending of your insanity.

Even though you will still be living in a world of insane people, you will notice that in order to get along with others you will probably have to *be* insane; yet you will see it as you are doing and observing it. You might even say to yourself, "There I am being insane again." without any sadness or remorse or attachments, and you will notice insanity each time it is happening.

It is true that you end being insane the instant you say that as a 100 percent truth, but essentially it doesn't knock down the entire wall. Speaking it does put a big hole through it. That hole is still surrounded by all the things you have built in your life which made you insane. It is like having a whole house built on toothpicks. You knock down a lot of toothpicks, but the house doesn't fall all at once. It sways and teeters and falls slowly. In a psychological fashion you would say "there it is—the insanity" each time you see it happening. When you speak from a place of clarity, you end insanity. Then, there is the *being* of it that comes along to show you all the places that you were insane, and if you accept them, you become insane again.

If in the moment you see you are insane, say it, and in that moment insanity ends in you. When it comes up again, which it will, acknowledge that is what you used to be, which is telling the truth about it. Just acknowledge it as *what was*. You will continue to have actions which are insane, for that is what you have been conditioned to be. Once you see your insanity 100 percent, it ends; yet there is a residue left. You have lived all your life in a certain way, so you are used to it that way.

For example, you may be right-handed, and then you sprain your right hand and it hurts to use it. You will probably continue trying to use it and realize it hurts. You will then use your left hand, thereby strengthening your left hand so that it becomes more normal to use it. Similarly, you have lived a life of insanity, and once you are sane you will still fall back on your insane actions, yet it will be obvious and you will notice it. Acknowledge the truth in the moment it happens as that is what you used to be, and then you will switch to being sane again.

If you see that you are insane and continue to keep being that, you will continue to use the old muscles, and you could possibly shift yourself back into being insane all the time. This happens to many people who have had an enlightening/transformational experience which only lasts a short time. They find themselves back in the insanity. You might know what I am speaking of as it has probably happened to you. It is easier to fall back on what you have always done. It is like the muscle builders who need to keep developing the weak muscles so those will be as strong as their other ones. They look for the muscles that are not as strong and work them. Noticing when you are not living in the moment will keep you living in the moment. This will bring your awareness to the moment, to the now.

Keeping Your Word

In the domain of speaking truth, our strongest muscle is lying. That is what we will use automatically because lying is the default pattern.

Being truthful comes down to keeping your word. Not your parents' words or your children's words, but *your* word. It is sometimes difficult to be consistent when you act and speak out of anger or any strong feeling. For example, you might be angry at your children and give them an unreasonable consequence. This is why I suggest you do not speak to children of consequences until you are calm and do not have any feelings attached. In that situation you could say to them that you realize you gave them and unreasonable consequence for their actions, and that was your mistake. Then go on to give them a reasonable consequence for the situation. It is important for you to first apologize for your mistake and possibly use it as a way to show them when someone is angry or having other strong negative feelings that they do not act rationally; that they are not sane. That is keeping your word to be in partnership with your children.

When you give your word by telling someone you will be there in 10 minutes and something comes up and you cannot make it, call the person and let them know. You don't need to have an excuse or make up a reason. Just let them know you will be late. You might realize when you gave your word that you were not aware something conflicted with it and that the time might need to be changed. That is still keeping your word if you change the time and you let them know. You do not need to add anything more or give an excuse for it.

There might be a situation where you need to make restitution for something you gave your word for that you can no longer do. For example if you tell someone you will be somewhere to assist them with something and you can't, you could find someone else to assist them. Always you need to realize it was your mistake and let them know that as well. Then be consistent by staying with whatever new arrangement you made.

Sometimes you might say something and then realize you were speaking from fear, obligation or guilt. When you realize you did that, apologize to the person and let them know what you really care to do or say. Sometimes not being able to keep your word is the best thing that could happen because then you can see yourself and the things you do to make excuses.

Be Free—The Good-Bye Exercise

Do this if you care to: Close your eyes. Now who's the first person who comes to your mind? Say the name and then say "good-bye" to that person using their name. Keep doing this until you cannot think of anyone else. Then say a "good-bye" to everyone you have ever had any relationship with. Include saying "good-bye" to any and all illness you have had, any and all pain, any and all suffering, any addiction you have or had, any and all anger, etc. After that is complete, notice how you feel inside. If there is anything other than calmness or peace, look at what is causing the discomfort, and say "good-bye" to that as well.

A two-fold action takes place when you do this exercise even though you may or may not notice it yet. First, by saying "good-bye" to them you have cut the cord; you have released them from bondage to you. That is a magnanimous act because in doing this you allow them to be free. And, secondly, it did the same for you. You gave *free,* so you get *free* in return.

I am not talking about freedom because freedom is something you have to defend and fight about. Free is not that. Free is the absence of attachments. Attachments are the labels we place on another and the manipulations we use to keep others in our lives. We often think of these manipulations as a good thing, such as doing things for them; yet those things are still manipulations and attachments.

From the standpoint of caring or giving or compassion, doing the "good-bye" exercise is the greatest gift you can give to anyone, which is for them to be free. That is where a partnership begins, from the place of everyone being free. You no longer have a daughter or son or husband or wife or friend or any of those roles and labels in your life. This does not mean you didn't give birth to a child. It doesn't mean you don't have others in your life. It just means that the child or partner or friend does not belong to you. You now have the real entities that can be in your life as themselves. This is allowing them and you to be free.

Love is not what we have been told and believe it is. Love is being free of attachments. We were taught by others and all the movies we watch that love is about having attachments, of having ownership over another. That is what marriage is. That is not love. It is ownership, and that is an attachment. It is not negative to have someone in your life; it is only negative when you attach to them, for then all your sadness, your suffering and your happiness are connected to that person and vice versa.

The essence of raising a sane child is to have a free person raising them. A free person doesn't say "my child" because using the word *my* creates an attachment. To be free means to have no attachments; and when you have no attachments, you will feel calm, possibly like you are floating.

For some of you, what I say here might cause you to be afraid when you think of not being attached to anyone or anything. On one hand, that is what you are probably seeking; and yet on the other hand, it means that you will be on your own and totally responsible for yourself. That can be scary. It will cause you to finally have to grow up. You are all stuck at age four. You have been attached to so many people for all of your life that you think you need attachments, and you don't know what it will be like without them.

You might even resist doing any of what I speak about because you believe you must have these attachments in order to have those people in your life. You might believe that without the attachments no one will be there. Yes, that is the risk that comes with being free, the risk that you might end up alone, and maybe you can see that you are already alone anyway. We are scared to death to discover that we are alone. The circumstances will not change about you being alone because that is what is true. You might think you are never alone since others are always on your mind. Yet, you are alone, and others being on your mind is the weight that is holding you from being free. You can hold onto them and be alone, or you can let them go and be alone. The distinction is that one *alone* is suffering, miserable, and painful, and the other *alone* is free. When all attachments are dropped, you will be free to discover the real you.

Most people never see the truth of *free* until just before they die. I am offering this to you so that you can experience it now and be able to live a life that is free rather than having one of pain and suffering, only to find out on your death bed it could have been different.

You might do the "good-bye" experiment once and discover that is all it takes to release the cords, or you might have to do it many times. You might notice you are holding on to someone again; and if so, then you just let them go anew. You will know if you are holding on as there will be either happiness or sadness when they are around or even when you think of them. Both happy and sad go together, yet you usually only feel one at a time. Either one shows you there is an attachment. If you feel anger, that is part of sad as sadness is hidden behind anger. You can either hold on, or you can be free. You cannot have your cake and eat it too.

If you are free, you are 100 percent responsible for yourself, which is putting yourself first. That is not being selfish. A selfish person would manipulate and control others. Someone who is not selfish gives *free* to everyone else first.

The selfish person says "I need to help them. They cannot make it without me, and I need to give them money. I want them to be happy, so they need to do what I say." That is how we control and manipulate people into staying in our lives.

The non-selfish person says "here, I am giving you free. Be the person you are."

As long as you don't let them go, you are forcing them to be the person you want them to be. You think that if they are just like you want them to be, they will be happy; but even though you think you want them to be happy, it is really you who wants to be happy.

You are not happy, and you think if they are happy then you will be happy. You also think they will be happy if they live as you think they should live; and since your life isn't happy, unhappiness is actually what you give to everyone you are holding on to. See how crazy this is. Do you really want to continue living this way?

Remember, happy is half of sad, and they are always together. If you want others to be happy, you are also asking them to be sad. If you really cared for someone, wouldn't you prefer them to be free? If you care for them to be free, then release them.

We quickly teach our children to be dependent on us. We even do this with others in our lives, and some people cannot give up that dependency. They want people to want and need them. Sometimes we don't really want the children to grow up. We want to keep them that tiny little baby who depended on us.

The only way to be free is to not be connected to anyone or thing—to have no psychological attachments. The speaking of letting someone go, as in the "good-bye" exercise, is the letting go. The act of speaking is the act of creation. It may need to be done just once, or you might need to state it anew as things reappear in your life and you notice them. You might see that you are manipulating or controlling someone and say "good-bye" to that as well. It is always best if you catch it as it is happening, in *the now;* and if that is not possible, do it when you can or when you become aware of it.

No Excuses

There is a story about Thomas Edison failing 1000 times in inventing the light bulb. He said he didn't fail 1000 times. He said he found 1000 ways that will not work. The key is that he didn't give up; he kept doing it until he finally did invent the light bulb. He would not have gotten to the invention of the light bulb without the failures. Often you experience one failure and give up and quit. If you take responsibility for each of the failures, and acknowledge them as failures, it leaves a little space you can move into. If you don't acknowledge your failures, you are doomed and destined to keep repeating them as there is no space to move in a different direction.

If you make excuses for the failure, that is the same as giving up. Even worse, since it is then almost impossible to see the failure, you say "I didn't do this or that because. . .," and that *because* causes you to not acknowledge it and to not take responsibility for it which leaves it hanging there to be repeated. People keep asking why they keep getting the same problems or why something keeps happening. The answer is that they hadn't acknowledged the failure and accepted the responsibility for it happening. They failed and they will blame and complain and use every excuse for it; then complain and blame and make excuses when it happens again and again. Some people have hundreds of excuses for their one failure and then wonder why they are in so much pain and suffering.

Instead of coming up with excuses and giving up, simply state "I have failed." The act of speaking, which is linguistics, is creation, and creation starts when something ends. In order to create something new, the old must end. Speaking it ends it and leaves a space for something new to come in. In order for the act of creation to happen, you must speak the truth. The truth in this case is that you failed. If you are speaking excuses or blame or justifications, that is not creation since they are lies you have used to cover up the failure. Those are ways to hide behind what is true. We feel that mistakes are a bad thing, and we live our lives in fear of making them, so we hide them. Yet, the truth is that living involves making mistakes. If you aren't making mistakes, you aren't living. So, instead of fearing mistakes or failures, you need to look forward to making them, so to speak. In each instance of the failure just say "I failed." Then there is that space for a new possibility to manifest.

Stand Up and Get Moving

Be active in your transformation, not passive. Don't just sit back and read some gurus and repeat what they say and wait for years for something to happen. Experiment with life. Be aware of your thoughts and what is going on around you. Active participation in your own transformation is what is needed. Transformation is often not a big bang that just happens. It is something we do to create it, and the first ingredient to transformation is speaking the truth.

In my life, I was always looking for the truth. I was not seeking transformation or enlightenment. The only thing that made a difference to me was the truth. Did I take the quarter? Did I eat the last cookie? Did I speak the truth of my actions?

When I failed at something, I didn't make excuses for it. I said, "I failed." I saw that it was me, not someone or something else. I took 100 percent responsibility for whatever and everything that happened in my life. Admitting failure is very difficult.

Our world wants to make excuses, and everybody wants to say "oh, don't call it a failure." They don't see that unless and until you do call it a failure, it will continue. We don't ever see it for what it is, so we keep repeating it. If we see failure as it was or as it is, we don't repeat it, for it is completed by speaking the truth of it.

Some people give up when they have a failure. Saying that you have failed is completing it which leaves a space for something new to come. Saying that you have failed and that you give up is not ending it, so the failing will continue. In saying that you gave up after you have admitted your failure, anything you add such as an excuse or reason will cause the failure to continue.

Sometimes it does take some effort to do all these things. I am not going to say it is easy even though it could be the easiest thing in the world. Transformation can happen in quantum, without any time at all, or it might take many, many years. For most, it is a matter of getting out of your comfort zone—that place where you live. Many people may not really be very comfortable; yet what is familiar seems to be comfortable. Making a shift like that often does take effort and sometimes it even works.

If you are stuck in a rut, it might take some effort to climb out. Often people get almost to the top and then fall back down again, and it seems like getting out is taking much longer than it needs to. That is OK. Keep on going with it, and when you get to the top, kick the ladder away so you cannot get back down. If you cut the cords to everyone, as in the "good-bye" exercise, you no longer have other people to depend on, and your life is totally up to you. You will have to get out all by yourself, and that is the only way it can be.

If you get the context of what I am speaking, then you will get to the content. The content is infinite, and then you could be looking at it forever, never seeing the forest for the trees. You can never put Humpty Dumpty together again from the pieces. That is what traditional psychology and psychiatry are based on—working on the content.

If you create a context, which could be to allow everyone in your life the space to be free, you will notice when that is not happening. You will notice when you are controlling, manipulating or have any other attachment to them. That is living from the context rather than the content.

You can create a context for whatever you care to have, such as creating a partnership or creating transformation, and that can start with simply saying "I create a partnership with myself" or "I create transformation." Then anything that isn't either of those will be easy to spot as you watch your life. When something that is not a partnership or transformation does pop back up, notice it, let it go and possibly say your creation anew.

The crux of everything I have ever spoken about and what we can do not only for ourselves but also for our children and those people around us to bring forth a new human being is tied to linguistics and speaking truth. Linguistics, the aspect of speaking as well as listening, is the key to being free; to being a new human being if free is what you care to be.

www.ingramcontent.com/pod-product-compliance
Lightning Source LLC
Chambersburg PA
CBHW051636050426
42443CB00025B/399